Nurturing Love

Nurturing Love

A Guide to a More Peaceful Marriage

*A handbook for
the heart and soul*

Salima Sanford

Mistletoe Press

Design by Meadowlark Publishing Services.

Cover and interior illustrations by Patty Schork Wear.

Author photo courtesy of the author.

Published by Mistletoe Press.

Manufactured in the United States of America.

ISBN 979-8-9855111-1-6

Published 2023

Contents

Contents

Preface

I have written this book as a plea for us all to be more loving in our marriages. In striving to give loving-kindness, we will need to tap into our divine essence, and so will experience the holiness we all carry. In the giving of greater love to our spouse, we are transformed. Instead of waiting to be loved, complaining we are not loved, or trying to make someone else be more loving, we simply, repeatedly, graciously give love, overlooking our prejudices and our need for the other to be *deserving*. We learn to drop our arrogance, our certainty, and our imagined plans to simply become more loving, to the best of our patience and ability.

When I look back at my words in this manuscript, a part of me thinks, *What a lot of trouble this must seem*, to blindly trust with no guarantee of reward. Yet in my hope for more peace in my household, in my desperation and fatigue, I determined to trust. I established new habits that helped me subdue my ego and give love even when it was hard. I never realized how it would transform me, my spouse, and our marriage. The results have been life changing.

Here are the truths I uncovered and the pledges I made:

I cannot live with anger any longer.
I accept that God wants me in this marriage.
I will honor God in my words and deeds.
I will give, to the best of my ability, uncon-ditional love and kindness.

How to begin to give the unconditional love that honors the sacred bond of marriage is the subject of *Nurturing Love.*

Introduction

Respect other people's ways and do
not disdain anyone's existence.
In the beginning is kindness, in the
end, forbearance and gentleness.

With the advent of Covid came greater isolation, creating new challenges in all our relationships, including those with ourselves and with God. Spending more time with our spouses and intimate family, we may have wanted more from them. With seemingly fewer opportunities to love and be loved, our aloneness might have turned to loneliness. In addition, unkind actions appeared to be more prevalent worldwide, laying another weight upon our hearts, and leaving us with far more questions than answers.

How can we nourish our hearts, restore our faith, and sanctify our relationships, especially the relationship of marriage? Is there something we can do to soothe and ease our feelings of separation, some salve for the loneliness, grief, and frustration we sometimes feel? I believe there is. Our saving grace comes in the embodiment of the unconditional love of which we all are capable. Like the magic penny in the childhood song, *Love is something if you give it away, you end up having more.*

In my previous book, *Healing Your Marriage by Healing Yourself,* I shared suggestions for finding peace in intimate relationships. Many found it helpful, but eventually, due to the strong challenges of my own marriage, I was led to uncover deeper truths. Surely the volatility of my relationship with my husband could be healed. With a steadfast commitment to this belief and continued spiritual walking, a series of truths slowly unfolded for me. These truths led to an acceptance of, and eventually gratitude for, my situation, and the discernment of a clear direction for my efforts. As a result of a few major perceptual shifts, which I share in the chapters to come, and a dedication to learning how to love, I began to taste the peace, love, and safety that are available for everyone in a committed union.

A Walk Through This Book

This book is about the how and why of cultivating love. Softening your habitual way of relating to your spouse requires dedication. Because your gestures may be barely noticeable at first, consistency and conscientiousness are needed. Your efforts to be a caring mate must issue forth from a place deep inside, the place of silent conversation between your two souls. You will be exercising new spiritual muscles, an effort beginning with hard work but ending in passionate desire. Be advised, this text is not about your getting what you think you want in your marriage. It is about opening to the possibility of something bigger and more wonderful than your imagination could dream.

Part One addresses the foundation of the work: infusing your relationship with loving-kindness. It introduces this concept, asks you to consider your commitment to your marriage, and encourages you to anticipate the subtle shifts that will come to your relationship when you, as half the marriage equation, change your own perceptions and priorities. Hope is given in the exploration of the truth of the divinity we all carry. Help is given for resolving the dilemma of how to care for your spouse and your spiritual practices at the same time, especially when your differences are magnified.

Part Two describes the art of practicing unconditional love and the transformation it brings. It addresses the difficult work of facing the "hard stuff" in a marriage and includes both stories of success in this endeavor and cautionary tales. It emphasizes the benefits of shifting from blame and criticism to self-responsibility and healing.

Part Three presents a key ingredient to the lessening of conflict between husband and wife interpreted from thirteenth-century Sufi mystical teachings. It also suggests several supportive practices and important qualities that you may consciously cultivate as your marriage and your experience of it begin to transform.

.　　.　　.

Whatever the nature of your current relationships, particularly the bond with your spouse, it is my prayer that you find help and motivation within these pages. I truly believe that applying these teachings can bring you to a place of deeper peace, love, and trust in your marriage.

Dear Lord, You are the Pen. I pray I may be the ink that flows from Your fingers.

Part One

1

Toward Loving-Kindness

*And join me to You
And remove Your veil of cloud
from my eye.
And place a barrier between me and
everything other than You.
And let nothing come between
me and You
And make me one of the leaders of
Your goodness and caring.*

Leaders of goodness and caring—quite an inspiration. The care and maintenance of loving relationships is a priority for us all, but also an area where our shortcomings are frequently revealed. What better avenue to learn about goodness and caring than through the intimacy of our closest relationships?

My focus is on marriage because, unlike our relationships with friends, children, or relatives, (with the possible exception of siblings), marriage is a bond that can support us for the rest of our lives, till death do us part. Strengthening this bond not only brings joy to a couple but actually creates an atmosphere of light and love that impacts everyone within close range.

Why else would you go to all this trouble? Because all marriages can use a boost, and because marriage is the best avenue for spiritual growth. Marriage offers love and challenges all in one package. We are given the opportunity to learn patience, wisdom, peace-making skills, trust, gratitude, and so much more. In a committed love relationship we are offered the chance to give of ourselves even when it is hard, which can transform us for the better in so many ways. Even our mistakes are our teachers, opening in us forgiveness and mercy as we make amends.

How are you with your marriage? Perhaps you have a pretty good marriage with no complaints, but a part of you longs for deeper intimacy or a revival of the ease and joy you initially had with your spouse. Maybe you have drifted into habits that simply need some readjustment, a course correction. You may wish to be more patient and more loving, but you'd like your partner to do the same.

Being truly caring involves setting positive intentions, seeking divine guidance, and being steadfast in your efforts. Let's start with your intentions.

If your intention is to stay married, I aspire to help you learn to love in a new way, in a manner that doesn't drain you but rather fills you up again and again.

Become kinder with every hour,
For every hour takes you closer to your
departure.

Love is its own compost; as we open a door to the flow of love, our capacity to love is not used up but rather grows and grows, being continually fed from Source. Love is our most precious gift, one that knows no limits. Just as you cannot touch without being touched, you cannot love without love's return.

Love is the life force in all creation.

Know, my beloved, that the love is eternal
between Allah and His creation and the
electric circuitry of His love flows through

everything. If not for this, nothing would move that moves; nothing would live that lives. Every planet in its orbit and every cell in its course is a witness of the love of Allah and a sign of His wisdom. Keep this love inside you and live with it all the time because the moment you lose it, you lose yourself; you lose Him.

As we learn to love more completely, our lives and the lives of those around us will be transformed. A quality of holiness surrounds us when we love. In an atmosphere of love, all opposites are united: good/bad, strong/gentle, believer/non-believer. Our differences melt in the Oneness born of practicing loving-kindness.

A Prayer for You ...

Dear God, help us feel the love that You have woven into the very atoms of our being. Help us trust the nearness and immensity of your Love for all of creation, including our imperfect selves. Help us become more generous of heart, for Your sake. Forgive our mistakes, and strengthen us in the capacity for tender, fearless love. Shower Your blessings upon all our relationships, and especially upon the sacred bond of marriage.

Help us as we discover our next steps toward becoming more loving partners. We pray for Your support and guidance in our efforts. May You be the Light upon our path and our Friend should we stumble.
In Your Name we pray,
Amen

2

Laying the Foundation

*That part of your life that has gone by
is irreplaceable, and that which has
arrived is priceless.*

Now is the time to nurture love. If we are to live in an atmosphere of peace and fulfillment, we must learn how to honor, fortify, and nourish our existing bonds of love, especially the bond of marriage. Women particularly need the surety and safety of a home base in order to move out in the world carrying the love, forgiveness, peace, and wisdom that are their inheritance. To fulfill themselves, men too benefit from the trust, respect, and love that marriage can provide.

You may already be making an effort to be loving and kind, but we can always do more. Implementing a program of loving-kindness may sound simple, but putting it into daily practice may require changing your habitual ways of relating to your spouse. Patience, dedication, spiritual support, and inner strength will all need to be rallied.

To begin with, let's consider our habitual patterns. We may all recognize an aspect of ourselves in this tale of Nusruddin, a Persian Sufi folk character.

Mullah Nusruddin and the Cheese Sandwiches

One day, Mullah Nusruddin opened his lunch bag at work and complained, "Another cheese sandwich! I'm so sick of this!"

Then the following day, yet again Mullah opened his bag and alas, he said, "Cheese sandwich! I hate cheese sandwiches! Oh, why, God? Why is it always a cheese sandwich?"

Finally one of his coworkers asked, "Mullah, why don't you tell your wife you don't like cheese sandwiches?"

Mullah replied, "But I don't have a wife."

His coworker confusedly asked, "Well, then, who makes these cheese sandwiches?" "Well, I do!" Mullah replied.

If you want your patterns of relating to your spouse to change significantly, you may welcome some help and inspiration. Perhaps you question the value of making an effort to be more loving when previous attempts have made little difference. I speak from my heart when I say that if there is still a place for love in your heart, *no effort is too great for the blessings that will come* as you begin to love your beloved in a new way.

> *When love beckons to you, follow him,*
> > *Though his ways are hard and steep ...*
> > *And when he speaks to you believe in him*
> > *Though his voice may shatter your*
> *dreams as the north wind lays waste the*
> *garden ...*
> > *But if in your fear you would seek only*
> *love's peace and love's pleasure,*
> > *Then it is better for you that you ... pass*
> *out of love's threshing floor,*
> > *Into the seasonless world where you shall*
> *laugh, but not all of your laughter, and weep,*
> *but not all of your tears.*

All marriages can grow in trust, peace, and love, but in order for change to happen, at least one of you needs to approach the relationship differently — that one would be you. It will be worth your effort. You can learn to actively love at a level that may seem beyond your capacity, a change in behavior that will yield rewards for both you and your mate. Your giving of unconditional love can lead to a unifying wholeness, a unity between you two. Moreover, in spending less time trying to control the relationship, you will have the time and temperament to take better care of your own needs, and so will grow in knowledge and appreciation of your best self.

With regard to marriage, some may be reading this book out of curiosity while others may be at their wits' end, contemplating separation or even divorce. I reached the point of separation several times because I could not find lasting peace with my husband; the tools I had been using had worked only to a point. I realized the reason they failed was that everything I was doing, with the best of intentions, had been about *me* and my needs. There had to be a major shift in my approach to the relationship: I needed to address God's needs.

The giving of love is transformative. The nicer you become, the nicer your spouse will be. Although renewal of trust may be slow, each day, each hour, brings positive change. In the meantime, you may ask, what about your needs? As the trust and love between you two grows stronger, you may be eager to speak to your spouse about what he or she could do better, but this is not yet the time. First you must lay the groundwork upon which a trusting and loving partnership can rest.

In marriage, we have so much to learn from one another if we can but allow ourselves to surrender. When we let go of our wants and let God give us what we need, miracles do happen. God has placed you in this particular marriage for a reason, and that is to bring you closer to your best self and closer to God, and to witness the creation of a more perfect union. The blessings of that long-awaited union can bring you to your knees in awe and gratitude.

I am asking more of you than, as a friend advised me, to see the good and ignore the unlikable qualities of your spouse. This is because the designation of your spouse's attributes as good or bad keeps you in judgment and prevents you from seeing deeper, into the realm of the possibilities that lie unacknowledged and unexplored within you both. Steadfastly giving your partner love will lead to your loving the whole of your spouse, unconditionally. In time, you will even find endearing the behaviors you used to object to.

It will be helpful to begin by appreciating *yourself*. You may have walked through some tough and challenging times, yet you are still trying to honor your vows and make the best of your marriage. Accept the limitations of your humanity and honor the sincerity of your efforts. Set aside time to feel God's appreciation of you. That feeling of appreciation from on high is the greatest reward for your efforts to be more loving, bestowing upon you an assurance of your inner goodness.

Dedication to nurturing love is not a quick fix, but rather a lifelong change in how you relate to your spouse. This is both easy in its simplicity and difficult in the doing. If you are to step into a greater capacity to love unconditionally, you will need help: not so much from well-meaning friends and family but from God.

With the best of intentions, friends and family may remind you of all the difficulties you have endured in your marriage, thus creating doubt in your heart and mind and keeping you in resentment of and separation from your mate. You may then begin to question the wisdom of putting all your efforts into a program of seemingly selfless giving. Why should you be so kind to someone who hasn't been kind to you? Shouldn't your spouse make an equal effort? The whole idea of giving without assurance of receiving, of changing your behavior because it is the right thing to do, may seem like too much trouble.

Yet what have you got to lose? Take this opportunity to polish your heart and soften your words and deeds. Help build a renewed atmosphere of love in your home. You will not be alone on this journey. In the chapters to come you will find guidance, cautions, and tales of success.

Truly I tell you, whatever you did for one of
the least of these brothers and sisters of mine,
you did for me.

Our words can create separation between us
and others—or they can erase all separation. Here
are some examples of the power of our thoughts
and deeds.

I had a friend who taught about love and kindness in a nearby prison. Each time she arrived at
the prison gate, she was confronted by an angry
female prison guard who alone had the power to
admit her, and who frequently created obstacles
to her entrance, always ranting angrily about one
thing or another. My friend was irritated by the
woman's interference and routinely objected. She
had the right to be peeved, but one day, tired of
it all, at the end of the guard's tirade she simply
said, "You're right." The guard was stunned, and
silent for some time, and then let her pass through.
After that, the guard put no more obstacles to her
passing through the gates. Since that day, had you
seen them together you would have thought they
were friends; and from then on, they were.

Even body language can turn hate into love.
My older sister's adult daughter was furious with
her one day, yelling across the room her objections
to something her mother had said. My sister was
about to object to the unfair accusations when she
heard a voice inside saying, *Give her a hug*. Against

her natural inclination, she crossed the room and embraced her daughter, even as angry as the girl was. In that moment the daughter's anger left her, leaving only tears and love in its wake. To quote my sister, "We took those words and threw them away. They were nothing. *I am here for you,* our bodies said, and we were just there."

In both cases there was a person filled with anger, an anger that melted away when they were given what they really needed—love and acceptance. Their neediness for love was manifesting in a manner that almost certainly assured their needs would not be met. It is not uncommon for persons needy of love to drive others away with their words. Fortunately, both my sister and the woman who taught in the prison felt behind the words that had been thrown at them, reaching the person's cry for love and responding to that instead.

These examples show that giving love, without judgment and regardless of the behavior of another, can heal the wounds of separation. The ultimate and most painful separation is from God. Unconditional love can heal this separation as well.

Even our thoughts have the power to uplift or bring down another, as they carry expectations for the other's behavior, whether positive or negative. We expect meanness from someone and we see it manifest. We expect lack of competence in someone and it manifests. Something similar

happened with a group of students whose teachers who were given false IQ scores for them. Over
the course of the year, the students given high fake
IQ scores outperformed students given low fake
scores, but not because of any conscious actions
on the part of the teachers. This underscores the
power of our judgments, even when unspoken or
unacknowledged.

> *You cannot separate the just from the unjust*
> *or the good from the wicked, for they stand*
> *together before the face of the sun, even as*
> *the black thread and the white are woven*
> *together.... And when the black thread breaks*
> *the weaver shall look into the whole cloth, and*
> *he shall examine the loom also.*

When we judge someone to be wrong, this is
even more reason to give them loving-kindness,
showing both forgiveness and another way to be.
Do we not also make mistakes? As you give unconditional love, you create an atmosphere of love,
which will change your feelings toward yourself,
toward others, and toward God.

> *Things that happen to us are not meant*
> *to make us feel guilty or accuse us of our*
> *mistake. Everything comes from a deep, lov-*
> *ing care. Therefore, when you are exposed to*
> *the storms of life, know that everything only*

serves to open your heart and widen your consciousness, giving you the opportunity to go through the fear and to become free.

Let's examine how we deal with discord. Although a part of us is always aware when we are not at our best, we may lay the blame on others, particularly those we live with. We may even demand that they change so that we can be nicer. Be reminded, the troubles in our relationship are not really our spouse's fault. God does not ask us to abandon ourselves or to be a martyr, but only to be kind, to do unto others as we would have them do unto us.

The medicine for our resentment and frustration lies within the choices we make. If what we want is sweetness, kindness, and gentleness, we must be sweet, kind, and gentle. Yet offering unconditional love does not mean being a doormat. It does not mean allowing someone to treat us poorly, but our objection to what our spouse does must first be taken to God. In the heat of the moment, you cannot understand the whole of any event. You may never understand the whole of an event, certainly not as seen through God's eyes. When irritation comes, take some time away for self-healing so you can return to love.

It would be more pleasant if your beloved's uncomfortable words or seeming abandonment never touched those tender parts of your wounded self. But this is not what God intended. God loves you so much that He wants you to be the best you can be. He wants to help you find, purify, and let go of the wounds you are protecting. If someone touches those places of sensitivity, be assured that God's presence and support are right there. This knowing allows you to be part of a much bigger container, of which your hurt is only a part. Knowing this truth mitigates your feelings of separation from God. God is present in our fortune and our seeming misfortune. Reflect upon this truth.

God brought you this spouse who can sometimes appear unlovable or unloving so you can better know and polish your innate goodness and begin to taste love, mercy, and the sweetness of patience. God allows your experience of hardship, often through loved ones, so you might recognize what lies inside you that is ready to be released, so that in your neediness, you will seek God's help. The big question being asked of you is this: Can you love God even in the seeming imperfection of life's most challenging events?

Loving our spouse when the relationship becomes difficult requires us to choose love over what we think we want. When seen through the eyes of your heart, your spouse will always be lovable. Why? Because you have loved him or her when it was not easy, and thereby have begun to know unconditional love, and to experience the deeper connection of your souls.

Love is too powerful to be kept in the confines of the heart.

The truth is that as you practice love, your love for your spouse will grow. The more you love him or her, the more love will flow through you from the infinite Source, and the more love you will eventually receive. Your partner may not love you in the way you would have asked for, or even imagined, but you will recognize it as love as you come to know the heart from which it blossomed.

Be assured that in the safety of your love, your mate's love for you will begin to emerge. All humans want to love and to be loved. *Be the love.*

In the next chapter you will be challenged to fully commit to your marriage if that is your guidance. This commitment is the rock upon which a new creation will be built.

3

Commitment to
Your Marriage

*And ever has it been that love knows
not its own depth until the hour of
separation.*

It is time to seek divine guidance regarding your commitment to your marriage, and to receive it through your heart, not your mind. Your connection to God will be the foundation for your decisions to come, so as you consider your commitment, you want to be fully present, free of distraction, and in a prayerful state. The following meditation is designed to help you enter this state.

A Meditation ...

Allow your mind to soften. Take some time to sit in silence, connecting as deeply as you can to that still, small place within. Observe the quietness that surrounds you and fills you as you still your mind.

Breathe in. Breathe out. Ride your breath.

Bow your head and your mind to your heart, and gently, slowly, move your consciousness from your head to your heart center. Let yourself experience the grace and wisdom that lie within.

Breathe in. Breathe out.

You are a body of light. Connect your heart's light to the light that surrounds you. Feel that light expanding until it has no limits. Feel its vastness. Breathe.

Breathe in the love and breathe out whatever stands between you and your awareness of the truth within.

Sit quietly for a few minutes more, readying yourself to look honestly at your marriage.

O children of Adam, as long as you invoke only Me, pray only to Me, and place all your hope only in Me, I will forgive whatever you have done, and I will not consider it any fur-

ther. O children of Adam, even if your errors reached as high as the clouds in the sky and yet you asked for My forgiveness I would forgive you. O children of Adam, if you came to Me with as many sins as the earth could hold and yet would meet Me without recognizing any other source of power, I would meet you with an equal amount of forgiveness.

God's mercy precedes everything. Let the God of love and mercy lead you to the truth. In the peace and quiet of your breath, your mind can become the servant of your heart's knowing.

A Prayer for You ...

Dear Lord, thank you for all the joy-filled blessings in my life and all the challenges that test me and remind me of my neediness for You. I come to You today, in sincerity and humility, asking from the core of my being for Your guidance regarding my marriage. Help me open the ears of my heart and my soul that I may know Your truth. Is it in the highest for me to remain in this marriage? Is it your wish? Please show me a sign or let me hear Your guidance.
Amen

You need certainty about God's will for you. Is staying in this marriage the loftiest decision, or

is God opening another door for you? You may
already know you want to stay married, but it will
still be helpful to feel God's blessing and pleasure
at your decision. Knowing God cares and supports
you will make easier the work to come.

God speaks to us through our hearts, so let your
heart be your guide. That which feels good in its
imagining is more likely to reflect God's will than
a choice that leaves you feeling bad.

A Practice: Consider Your Commitment

If you are certain of God's will for your marriage,
you might want to skip to the prayer near the end
of this chapter on page 29. But if you are still in the
decision phase, here are some points to consider.
You may wish to take some notes as you explore
the following:

First, *fully imagine breaking off the marriage,*
whether in the short or long term. Picture
yourself walking out the door and starting a
new life without your spouse. Acknowledge
all the thoughts that come up.

You may feel a sense of freedom at first:
freedom from the duties and challenges of
your marriage, freedom to become who you
truly are. Honor each thought. Ask yourself what voices propelled those thoughts:
for example, "I'll never be happy in this

relationship." "I no longer feel love for my spouse." "I want to find myself."

Of course you have a choice, but remember: your doubts and desires are clues to parts of yourself that will eventually need to be revisited and healed, regardless of whether you stay or go. Your feelings of lack regarding happiness, love, peace, or self-fulfillment may well be exacerbated by the presence of your spouse, but those feelings were already present inside you. Perhaps this marriage, or the next, could be the very vessel that leads to the dismantling and release of these painful feelings of deficiency.

Recall the times you needed your spouse and he or she wasn't there for you. How did that feel? What might you have done differently to get your needs met? How could you have been a better mate? Do you have regrets for any of your thoughts or actions in this relationship?

Consider what you would miss if you left the marriage. What attributes does your spouse carry that you appreciate? For example, patience, steadfastness, common sense, diligence, mirth. Consider the best in your spouse. Recall the times you have needed him or her and your spouse was there for you. How did that feel?

If you have children, consider the current impact of your marital relationship on them (and even your beloved pets). If you separate, how do you anticipate they will be affected? It is important to find clear guidance because uncertainty about your relationship will be conveyed to your children by your very presence; other family members and pets, too, will resonate with what you are feeling.

Have you tried to break off the marriage before? What was your spouse's response? Often women encourage their husband to ask for a divorce because they don't want to be the ones to break up the relationship, but their husband does not budge. Why is that? Fear, maybe, but the more accurate truth is that his love has not died.

If you just aren't crazy about your spouse because he or she irritates you, and you are mad at God because you don't see any way out, it will help to let go of your pictures of perfection. The likelihood is that if God wanted you out of your marriage, it would have already ended. In truth, the decision is not really yours to make; we cannot hold on to that which God wishes to break, nor can we easily destroy what God decrees should remain.

To paraphrase a hadith,* *What hit you could not have missed you. What missed you could not have hit you.* Ease comes when a decision is the right one; we can sense when a door is open because everything falls into place. On the other hand, we can feel when the door to a choice is closed because no matter how hard we push for something to happen, our will does not prevail. Even when my own marriage hung by a thread, it was a thread made of steel.

This is the turning point for you as the reader. If you are serious and sincere, ask God this question: *Is it in the highest good for me to stay in this marriage?* If you need to sit with this question for a week, then do so, because everything that follows in this book is predicated on your knowing that God in His wisdom has given you this marriage.

On Guidance
You might be wondering how to find the truth and clarity of divine guidance. Consider each option and see how it lands on your heart, not in your mind. As you imagine each one, connect with God and with your inner knowing, and see how you

---

*   A hadith is a collection of traditions attributed
     to the prophet Muhammad based on his say-
     ings and actions.

feel. A choice in alignment with divine guidance will feel good; choices that diverge from that guidance generally leave us feeling uncertain, even guilty—there is no lightness to them.

God's orders come down much like light, or quietness, or certainty, or peace. Learn to recognize what this confirmation feels like for you. You might see an image or feel an emotion, a tingling, an inner strength. The way we experience guidance is unique to each of us. Truth just feels right, unwavering. Be wary of second thoughts that can pull you away from that initial feeling. This is the mind kicking in to override your true knowing.

Truth comes from that deep, still place in our spirit that just knows. Sidi writes, *You are the question and you are the answer*. When you feel the strength and certainty of your knowing, align with this truth. As you follow your guidance, be cautioned not to act beyond the original guidance that you divined. For example, the voice of truth might say, *You do not have to live with anger anymore.* But does the voice say *move out, get divorced, be hard on your spouse?* Perhaps not yet, but you can at least know with unalterable truth that you are done living with anger (or negligence, or whatever your red line may be).

Maintain your connection to God. It is easier to detect a false next step if you do. Maybe this first truth means that in the next year God will show you how to love in a way that mitigates anger, or maybe your divine guidance will be to move out for a short spell. You may not yet know. God will help us navigate even the toughest of situations if we but listen to His guidance at each step of the way.

If you do not feel the door is open for you to end this marriage, then assume that committing to your marriage is in the highest good for you, and that it is in God's plan. It may not make sense to you right now. This marriage might not be what you had pictured marriage to be, but there is a greater wisdom at work. For your growth and for your spiritual walking, this marriage may be just what you need.

Check in with your body, your heart, your spirit. Are they all in alignment with your decision? Do you feel clarity regarding your decision? Once more, sit with God and let the truth sink in. When you are certain and ready, make a vow to God regarding your choice.

A Prayer for You ...
(You may change "spouse" to "wife" or "husband" as you wish.)

> *Dear Lord, if it is in Your wish for me to be in this marriage, I will honor Your wish. Please guide me and help me treat my spouse in a manner that pleases You. Help me find You in him [or her]. Help me serve You through my spouse. Please forgive the times when I falter,*

*when I lose patience, when I am not kind,
because those times will come. Remind me to
sit with You each day and draw upon Your
strength, Your mercy, Your wisdom, and
Your goodness, for I need You. Help me come
to feel the pure joy of the goodness that will
grow in me as I strive to please You, in word
and deed, through my marriage. With you as
my witness, I promise to make this my goal:
to give my spouse abiding love, Your love, for
Your sake, and with Your help.
Amen*

Take a moment to journal on your reflections.

What's Next ...

Part of my healing began the day I faced my relationship to my marriage and asked God, *Do you
want me to stay in this marriage?* This time I *really*
listened for God's answer, in full surrender to His
will, as I could no longer bear half a marriage.
God's response was immediate. I felt the truth of
the light of the descension of a Yes. I knew in that
moment that this marriage was a gift from God,
and my heart broke open. The decision about the
marriage had never been mine to make.

Now that you have committed, let me speak
more about the nature of the gifts and challenges
presented in marriage. If God put you together, it
is probably because your souls and spirits are well

suited to one another. It is also possible, however, that your egos and hearts collide, the result of different wounding, histories, habits, and desires. If you want to live in the world of the soul and not be tossed about by your emotions or ego, let this marriage walk you into the world where you live closer to your truest self, closer to the union of your spirits, and closer to God.

Over time, the difficulties between you two will begin to fade. If this is who God chose for you, then embrace your spouse. Feel your gratitude to God. Even if you cannot yet see the wisdom in His choice, once you fully commit, you will feel God's support pouring in.

It is fatiguing to fight *what is*. Surrendering to what God makes for you brings ease. I pray that your marriage, your self-understanding, and your relationship with God expand and flourish as you accept the challenges of marriage and employ some of the suggestions I will offer in the remaining chapters.

Because shared stories are sometimes helpful, I'll share a bit of how I came to love more deeply. The counselors we sought for advice always said that my husband loved me. I believed them, but I could not feel it. I saw so many negative emotions in his face, his lips, the set of his jaw that I could not look him in the eyes. *How could that much love and that much anger coexist in one body?* I wondered. Then one day during a session, our counselor made me look into his eyes, and I glimpsed unimaginable love and need and hurt shooting like a bolt of light into my heart, pleading to find a landing place. Though I still had much to learn, I was left with the certainty of, if not access to, his love.

When my faith had deepened enough to fully sustain me, I knew that God would help me learn to love. Clearly God had ordained this marriage and so God would nourish it. Over the next several years, I slowly received the wisdom of how to tend to love as God would have me do. The two major understandings that evolved I share in this book. The first teaching came from an inner knowing. The other was derived from the thirteenth-century writings of a Sufi mystic, Ibn al-'Arabi.

Upon reflection, and with humiliation and regret, it now seemed that my impertinence, my lack of gratitude had been like that of a very hungry person in a grocery store declaring, *I'll only eat this or that, nothing else,* while God is saying, *This is your meal. This is My choice for your nourishment. This man will be your love to the end of your days. I want you to love this man because he is the partner I selected for you, even if you cannot yet see it.*

When you love your spouse, actively love them, they will begin to tend to you, and you each will come to see the inner beauty of the other. When you hold the mercy for your mate, you will more easily have mercy for yourself. You will begin to accept God's endless mercy and forgiveness for you, in spite of any ingratitude, willfulness, arrogance, or judgments on your part. Your sincere regret and humility will invoke the infinite mercy and healing light that your heart and soul truly need.

This may be the most important thing you do in your life: to love, actively love, an imperfect mate. When you do, your life becomes an ongoing prayer and you know that God is ever-present, even when *you* turn away.

We may be imperfect in our humanity, but we are perfect in our divine essence. I invite you to allow the challenges of marriage to polish the mirror of your heart so your godly self can shine forth.

A Prayer for You ...

Dear Lord,
You are my Sustainer, my true Source of Love and Goodness. I am so grateful for Your continued support and guidance for my efforts to be more loving in my marriage. I know my marriage is a sacred union because it has been made holy by Your blessing. Please help me accept Your love and hear Your wise counsel. Increase me in patience, mercy, and love, for

Your sake. Forgive any arrogance or lack of faith on my part. Please continue to guide me in my marriage that I may give the love in a manner that pleases You.

My Lord, I can never thank You enough.

Amen

4

Our Hidden Treasure

The light on your face,
You will take with you.
All else, your sorrows your joys
and all that you lay claim on,
You will beave behind
The light on your face,
That you will take.

We all carry divine light, "The light that dispels
the darkness, as if the darkness never was."
In every moment we are flooded with the light
of God's unlimited love. How do we open the

floodgate that we may receive our divine inheritance? Patience, sincerity, prayer, loving-kindness,
and gratitude are some of the keys to accessing
this light within.

As we set out to learn more about giving and
receiving love, it is vital to continually strengthen
our connection to the divine love within us, and
through this connection to honor the beauty and
majesty of our being and to nourish the love that
we carry. Should we doubt our potential, let's look
at some wisdom teachings regarding the jewels
within our being.

I was a Hidden Treasure; I loved to be known,
so I created the creation in order to be known.

God created us in His image that we might
mirror for Him some of His beautiful qualities
(see Appendix C for an introduction to the divine
qualities). From this mystical teaching comes the
understanding that we have within us a treasure of
godly qualities. From the twelfth century onward,
major Sufi texts of the great masters such as Ibn
al-'Arabi and Rumi have made frequent use of this
understanding in their mystical writings.

To paraphrase from the translator's introduction to Ibn al-'Arabi's *Ringstones of Wisdom*, every
divine quality represents a manner in which God
is present in the world. Not all of God is reflected
in our world, but all of creation as we know it

reflects aspects of God. The world as a whole reflects all the divine qualities, but it is only in the soul of humankind that the totality of the Spirit in reflected. This is our center, which we have the potential to fully realize; this is our divine essence. As the translator writes:

> *The spirit of man is none other than the Spirit of all things, because no aspect of the Spirit is absent from him.*

We perceive one another and bond with one another through the recognition of our shared qualities. We resonate with each other through the commonality of one or more qualities: love, truth, strength, or wisdom, for example. "It is the presences of the Names (i.e., qualities) that make possible the coming together of beings, allowing each identity to form a link with others without destroying its own selfhood." Even connecting with someone in anger is connecting through the mutual longing for a divine quality, such as love or safety.

> *Love exists as a fundamental hidden jewel in the creation, and there is nothing in existence that is not associated with it in one way or another.... The quality of love is present in the kernel of everything.*

To be understood, we must simply be who we

are and let that person shine forth. Our true essence is holy and undefiled. It may help to imagine seeing ourselves the way God the All Merciful sees us. God is not judgmental; rather, it is our own self who is critical. Within each of us is every attribute we seek, waiting to be awakened, strengthened, and made clear. Our life's work is to unveil and purify each aspect of that divine essence.

You are the treasure but bring forth the secret jewels that are inside you.

Realizing Your Divine Qualities

The more deeply we awaken and purify these divine qualities in ourselves, the more connected we feel to the rest of humanity. As we better understand ourselves through our exploration of these qualities, we also come to understand God at a deep and wordless level and begin to radiate the light of the qualities simply through our presence. And, of course, love is a quality that resonates powerfully in all of us, lending passion, devotion and motivation to every endeavor.

A Practice: Examine Self-Talk

How can you realize this potential? To begin with, examine your self-talk. Resolve to observe your thoughts during a single day. You might be surprised at the number of times you negate yourself in your thoughts such as *Everyone thinks I'm an idiot, or I can never get it right.* Are similar thoughts part of your inner dialogue? If you do notice negative self-talk, strive to eradicate the habit. It won't take long. As you notice each negative thought, remind yourself that not only is it false, but it is an obstacle to your stepping into the truth of your being. Positive affirmations help, but abandoning your negative thinking makes it much easier to get in touch with your unique gifts.

A Practice: Embrace Your Shadow

When you have pretty much eradicated negative self-talk, there is another activity that will enhance your self-acceptance, although it sounds contrary at first. Begin, slowly, to look at things you don't like about yourself, one quality at a time, and embrace each of these as a part of you. For example, *I'm uncomfortable in groups. I'm so forgetful. I get jealous of others.* Be gentle with the whole of yourself as you do this. Remember that it's not our places of perfection that others find endearing, but rather our unique imperfections. Allow your uniqueness to surface. Whether you stumble over your words, or don't dress like everyone else, acknowledge that aspect of you and let it be okay.

There may be traits you'd like to change, such as jealousy or gossiping, because you know they are blocks to love. Acknowledge your neediness and ask God for help. Follow a path that leads you to becoming your best self, but as you take each step, do not pretend to be other than who you are in the moment. When you accept your nature as it is, even as you strive to be your best version, you'll become more comfortable with yourself, and so will others.

A Practice: Allow for Change

It is also helpful to eliminate statements that permanently define us, such as *I always (do such and such)* or *I can never (embody a certain quality)*. Such thinking can imprison us in a stagnant and often false self-opinion. We are not static creatures, but rather are always evolving spiritually. So do not announce who you are, but rather be the son or daughter of your moment. A new creation can come for you in the twinkle of an eye.

Understanding Our Divine Nature

Until we are truly tested, we do not know our limits. An example is the story of a young newlywed man who invited his two divorced biological parents and their respective spouses to a Thanksgiving dinner at his house. Neither parent had communicated much in the twenty years since their divorce, so it was a brave thing for him to do, a decision wholly driven by the profound love his new marriage had ignited in his heart. At the last moment his wife became ill, so it was left up to him to prepare the whole dinner, clean the house, look after his daughter from his first marriage, and be congenial, which he accomplished.

When the day of feasting drew to a close, he was asked if he was exhausted from doing so much work. He related that, surprisingly, the whole experience had been exhilarating because he had never dreamt he was capable of carrying off such an occasion by himself. He had been stretched to his limit and had met the challenge with love in his heart. In addition, he said that the greatest gift of all had come at the dinner table hearing the kindness in the exchanges between his parents, something he had not witnessed since childhood. The manifest truth was twofold: love is contagious, and when we carry the love, we are capable of so much more than we can imagine.

Why love? Because God loved us first and wants to see that divine love in our reflection. We were created with love and mercy in every atom of our being. Every cell of our bodies vibrates with all the godly qualities, but love and mercy are paramount. We carry within us a divine essence, an intrinsic knowledge of love, forgiveness, wisdom, goodness, strength, tenderness, and more, in the purest sense. God wants to see in us these reflections of His divine qualities.

We can find manifestations of these attributes (qualities) in ourselves, admit where we fall short, and ask God for help. As we listen to divine guidance, our understanding and our witnessing of love, mercy, peace, and all our divine qualities will increasingly be shaped by God's template. For example, our understanding of love, kindness, and mercy will become fuller, richer, and closer to God's version. This happens through our being shown, for example, what love is and is not, as well as through our desire to be more loving.

The intention to strengthen your connection with the Divine is critical to the success of your endeavors to love more completely. In whatever manner is most comfortable for you, seek connection to your Higher Power, the One Whose guidance is pure, and Who will never abandon you. As your experience of God's presence increases, you will no longer feel alone but rather will come to know that you have an ever-present Protecting Friend (*al-Waliyy*). In addition, you will begin to feel God's gratitude (*as-Shakur*) for your efforts. As you enter the unlimited ocean of divine qualities—love, forgiveness, peace, dignity, purity, and more—you will want even more to be your best self.

Your Essence Is Inviolable

> *Like the ocean is your god-self;*
> *It remains forever undefiled.*

No one can know the truth of your being except yourself and God. Since no one else can enter that hallowed ground, it follows that no one can damage the essence of your being. Our bodies, hearts, even our souls and spirits may be disturbed by life events, but the core of our being runs even deeper. It is never changing. It is inviolable and eternal. Draw comfort from this knowledge. This is the place that will see you through tough times and guide you on your journey to know yourself and know your Lord. From this place you will begin to understand how to give and receive love.

Self-Care

Nourishing the depth and certainty of your relationship with God is foremost. Although healing your marital relationship will comfort your heart, you also must regularly go to the Source to replenish. You will need time alone, and in community, if possible, to feed your faith through whatever practices return you to your God connection, your "god-self," as Kahlil Gibran calls our divine nature. Seek to fill your heart with love so that this love, God's love, can overflow in abundance.

God asks us to care for ourselves first, to fill our heart with love and mercy so these qualities can overflow effortlessly onto others. When we can touch into the endless source of divine love, we give not from a place of emptiness, but rather from a vast wellspring of love inside.

We may want to care for ourselves and yet

have difficulty with self-appreciation, observing only where we continually fall short of our expectations. We forget that God's mercy is always there. We may have the mistaken notion that we shouldn't think well of ourselves, forgetting that the source of any and all of our good qualities is *not us*, but rather God, and therefore should be appreciated and honored, not underrated through false modesty.

Clearing the Veils to Love

A good friend who went on a forty-day silent retreat shared with me that her main takeaway was how incredibly much God loves us all. I am taking her word for that. How, then, do we open to receive this very treasure we yearn to discover and share?

> *Your task is not to seek for love, but merely to seek and find all the barriers within yourself that you have built against it.*

All beings are made in love and carry love. It is our task to remove the veils that obscure love. One of the most recommended practices for removing the blocks to love is to ask God for forgiveness, to be in repentance (*Tawbah* in Arabic). Asking for forgiveness is not just about regretting our mistakes; it is always helpful regardless of our degree of perfection. The practice of Tawbah is about the recognition that as humans we can always do better and that we can never thank God enough for His provision.

As we move along our spiritual path, we are continually getting to know the treasures and shadows that live inside us. One clue to understanding ourselves comes from the awareness that our current emotional state is often reflected back in others' reactions to us. For example, if we carry anger, even unacknowledged, others will sense our anger and pull back from us without even knowing why. The emotion will be palpable, like the feeling in the air when two people have been arguing. Sometimes anger shows up in others in order to teach us patience and mercy, but often, what we think is another's anger is but a reflection of our own. At the extreme, we might not even know we have anger roiling beneath the surface until someone comes into our life who strikes that chord of rage. Then it is important to give love and mercy to ourselves, and to know that God is with us, even in our rage, walking us toward understanding and healing.

It also happens that people will gravitate toward us when we are in a peaceful or loving state, even without our speaking. Some say that it is because of the greater light we carry as we cleanse the veils obscuring our divine essence.

Others recognize in us the peace or love that they, too, have within.

When one of our qualities is muddied due to anger, grief, or fear, we may not be aware of the degree to which it will resonate with that same muddiness in others. If we are unaware of our state of being, we may accuse the other of the negative resonance that we actually set off in the subtle worlds. It isn't fruitful to try to improve someone else's qualities — it's a waste of time. Instead, tune up to a higher vibration, and if the other person can accept the light of that quality, their spirit will vibrate in resonance.

You may find it difficult to be kinder and more loving if you routinely experience a lack of loving-kindness in others. Humans may not always be kind to you — or more accurately, may not appear to be kind — and their words, thoughts, and actions may hurt your heart. As you begin to strengthen your connection to God, the Most Kind, the Most Loving, your need of others will be less. As you take greater responsibility for your reactions to others, and acknowledge the mutuality of inter-personal relations, your wounds around love will heal, and your capacity to love and be loved will grow. Allow patience, sincerity, gratitude, and honesty to be your companions.

This is not an easy path. The misery we encoun-ter on the journey comes from fighting acceptance of, and lacking appreciation for, what we have been given in our intimate relationships, especially in the relationship of marriage. In essence, we are saying to God, You have made a mistake. It wasn't supposed to be like this. Yet "God does not burden any soul except with what it can bear." This is true, though sometimes we are stretched to our limits—especially when we add our own stuff to the equation. Ironically, it is when we collapse in defeat that we see the light of truth and are able turn from self-management to God management.

I can only say that nurturing love works. It will bring greater peace to you and allow your spouse to step into his or her highest self, by example. The transformation of your marriage may not be evident in a day, but it won't take years. Every day you will see a change for the better in both of you if you stick with a few elements that are simple to understand yet challenging to consistently implement.

Take some time now to jot down any resources, people, programs, and practices you find helpful for nourishing your heart and strengthening your faith. Make a commitment to employ these on a regular basis; set up a calendar to hold you more responsible. You will need the support as you move forward, for much will be asked of you ... and much will be given.

The Divine Quality of Forgiveness
If you wish to work with one of God's qualities for forgiveness, you may want to explore two divine names for the All-Forgiving—*Ghafur* and *Ghaffar*.

Ghafur penetrates and touches the deepest part of our heart, the place where our most grievous offenses, our greatest slips lie. Ghafur goes to the worst that was ever done to us...that which we thought was unforgivable.... The quality of forgiveness is like a soft, swathing cloak that protects your heart from hardening and separation.... To carry the quality of Ghafur means to open the eye of your heart and see the greater interlinking of all, even beyond the present moment. I can raise my head again because I have made space for forgiveness, because I can become connected again, step by step, and there will come a moment when I feel the dignity and the strength to love....

Human beings who carry the quality of ... Ghaffar are capable of forgiving faults; indeed, they do not even see them as such....

So learn to forgive those who have mistreated you, who did not understand you or failed to see you as you are.... Be kind to those who need kindness, letting them be carried by your dignity, your generosity, your loyalty, and your wisdom.

5

A Subtle Shift

*Among the signs of success at
the end is the turning to God
at the beginning.*

Most religious theology says we are to put no one before God. For years, this created a painful dichotomy for me as I tried to balance my two most important relationships: the one with God and the one with my husband. It can be very uncomfortable to have your feet in two different worlds that you cannot reconcile. If God is not a part of your spouse's language, this adds an additional challenge, as you won't be openly sharing most of your spiritual life with him or her. Even though you try very hard to be a good companion, your thoughts may often wander in other directions, leaving you not fully present in either realm.

You might feel like you don't get back what you are putting into your marriage, or wish to see more growth in your marriage and spiritual walking, not to mention having more time for self-care. Instead of oneness, all you see is separation. Setting the intention to *serve God through your spouse* may resolve this dilemma. This is different from worshiping your husband. It is different from acting out of fear or victimization. This is different from being a good spouse. This is loving your spouse as God asks you to love—unconditionally.

All your needs can be met in the container of service to God. You can love God *in* your spouse and love God *through* your spouse. You can serve God by tending to your beloved in a manner that will please God. You are merely returning love to its Source *through* the man or woman whom God has ordained for you. When your words, deeds, and thoughts for your spouse come from a desire to please God, everything you do becomes a prayer.

Think about it. God has said, *I want you in this marriage. I brought you this very person for your own good, even if you cannot see this truth. Care for your beloved as I would ask you to. Do this for Me.*

This puts an entirely different spin on the intent

of your actions, knowing you are loving for God's sake. You begin to feel your own goodness in caring for your spouse. This provides a rich opportunity to grow in loving-kindness, not because you want to be seen as a good person but because it feels so good to realize the true nature of your being.

Putting God first resulted in a subtle but powerful shift in my life. I moved from struggling to be a dutiful wife, which was primarily about *me*, to allowing myself to serve God through my husband. You can love God through your spouse in every moment. The two of you can become one within the container of God's love. It's wonderfully amazing. You can finally be with God *and* your spouse at all times, which is to say that your spirit can rest in God, and of course, finally, there is only God.

Respect other people's ways and do not disdain anyone's existence. In the beginning is kindness, in the end forbearance and gentleness.

Sometimes we are guilty of not really paying much attention to our spouse, especially if he or she has some behaviors we dislike. We don't, or won't, see the whole of our spouse. Not wanting or being willing to connect more deeply, we may routinely ignore what our mate is saying or doing unless his or her behavior pleases us. It's no wonder we lack the intimacy we want.

What I'm saying is this: Give your spouse your full attention and love, not necessarily more often, but more completely, more selflessly. Give the love that comes from the joy of loving God, pleasing God, and honoring your own godly nature. Your rewards will, in God's time, be beyond anything you might have asked for.

Don't worry about exhausting your supply of love. You will never run out of love when you are no longer loving from your self. The love you are learning to give is from God, flowing *through* you from an unlimited Source. This is a subtle but powerful difference. Be aware of and attune to the nature of your loving as you learn to navigate and nurture the unconditional love of which you are capable. Keep God ever present.

> *The soil of our mind contains many seeds, positive and negative. We are the gardeners who identify, water, and cultivate the best seeds.*

Our hours on the earth are precious. Wouldn't we feel better if we used them to awaken, nourish, and deepen the love we have for others? Isn't it more joyful to live in a world where we are doing our best in a way that feeds our heart and the hearts of others? Let our aspiration be this: to love God and to accept the return of God's love through our spouse.

We hold the medicine for our marriage. If we are more conscious in our interactions, softer in our words and touch, and aligned with God's will, we can taste the holiness of love. Love your mate as God would have you love him or her, and observe what happens, because miracles will surely come.

Practice unconditional love and you will begin to feel really good inside, as if God were smiling upon you. You will begin to enjoy giving loving-kindness to this familiar and sometimes even annoying person to whom you are married. Moreover, the more consistently you give your partner loving-kindness, unattached to outcome, the deeper and stronger will be your love for them. There are several reasons for this.

- Love begets love. It is its own compost. God will multiply your storehouse of love as you shower it on others.
- You will feel closer to God, as you surrender your will to His.
- You will feel better about yourself. Through the act of loving, you will love yourself and others more, and thus begin to cleanse any attitudes that were contributing to negative thinking.
- As you begin to find pleasure in service, your container will expand. Whereas before you came to the ocean of love with a cup, you now bring a bucket, and one day you will simply dive in.

We are needier than we are willing to admit. It was allowing myself to feel my incredible neediness for love that finally broke my heart open to *receive* love. I recall the very moment and sensation of my heart's breaking. My husband held me as I wept in the face of the beauty and majesty of the instant pouring of love into my open heart, as if cascading down through a huge crevasse. I wept for the pain of the time lost, for the years without tasting love, and I wept out of gratitude.

Cleansing tears will come as we heal because underneath our veils of protection lie layers of vulnerability and neediness for love. Into this recognition of our complete need, divine love will flow like a river. We *can* increase our capacity to love. While we may not sustain our efforts to love so purely all the time—being only human—we will inevitably build a greater stronghold of peace, love, and trust in our marriage upon the ground of our good intention, God willing.

Your spouse is a conduit to God. Speak to him or her as if speaking to God. Listen from your heart, beneath their words, into the heart and soul from which the words emanate, as if God were speaking to you and sending you a glimpse of your beloved's innermost being.

My experience was that the more love I gave, the more I began to see my husband as a person, one I didn't know well but was interested in knowing. I was astounded to observe his likes and dislikes through new eyes. I began to seek him out and enjoy his company, and he, mine. It was a natural outcome of the cleansing of negativity between us.

As we begin to feel God's presence and help, and gradually accept who our spouse is, we may become more curious about this person whom God has given us to serve. We may be surprised to notice what moves their mind and heart. These mysteries have been there all along, but our aversion to certain of their behaviors has veiled us from true sight. As the clouds of stale observations lift, a miraculous, foreign spirit emerges. Each moment can bring a new revelation. We find renewed pleasure in our dedication to love. Our lingering physical presence, our kind words, our time, given freely, give unimaginable comfort to our beloved. Trust, the key to a lasting marriage, is established and continually strengthened.

> *So love and keep loving, time and time again.*
> *For even in your forgetfulness, your heart*
> *does nothing but precisely that, whispering*
> *day and night, "I want to love."*

Stumbling Blocks

As I mentioned in the last chapter, in order to *be* loving, it helps to have felt love from those around us, especially in our formative years. Perhaps in our childhood, loving-kindness was seen as a weakness, our gentleness taken advantage of. As a result, we made a decision about loving-kindness, usually adopting one of two protective beliefs: *I must always be kind and helpful* or *kindness is a sign of weakness.*

If we lacked that essential love as a child, to whatever degree, even now we may not trust the kindness of others, associating love with pain and disappointment. It may be difficult for us to receive love, having closed off our heart for protection. We could even be angry at God, feeling that He owes us something for the hardships of our childhood. We may insist on being loved *first* before we'll venture to give of our love.

As adults, not having felt nourished by love in our childhood, we may look extensively to others to fill that void in our heart, and inevitably come up short. Our need may be too great for anyone to satisfy. A woman recently shared with me that her ex-husband told her there was no point in being nice to her because she was a bottomless pit of need. Unable to meet her insatiable need, he had given up trying.

The tendency to close off parts of our heart does not mean something is wrong with us. If each of us examined our relationship to love, we would all find a point beyond which we cannot currently open to receive any more. Just as our heart feels pain when it is hurt, we also may feel pain in the presence of a greater love than we have felt before.

This entire discussion of giving generously of love may disturb pockets of unacknowledged anger, grief, or fear that you've carefully ignored. Now is a renewed opportunity to discover and welcome those emotions. As in the Rumi poem "The Guest House," these awakened visitors may be "clearing you out for a new delight."

The good news is that giving to please God reprograms our attitudes toward love. Through our efforts to give love, we begin to receive love, for who can resist loving-kindness given with no strings attached? By nurturing love, both parties are enveloped in God's gentleness and showered in goodness and mercy.

I invite you to love your spouse, not for who you assume them to be, based on your pictures, but for the mystery and holiness of this person's godly being, however unrealized.

At one time or another we've all been attracted to something whose outward appearance does not appear valuable. For example, you may treasure a primitive-looking clay figure your mother made—not because of its perfection but because it holds a connection to something deeper that mysteriously feeds your soul. It isn't the clay figure itself that moves your heart but rather something eternal it represents, perhaps a quality such as capability or grace. The outer form of the object awakens in you the memory of that quality in the woman

Clay figure by Evelyn Shelby Reed.

whose hands formed the clay. In the same way, you can begin to see beneath the appearance, habits, and deeds of your spouse to that unique divine essence that you sometimes glimpse: an essence that contains the same potential as you have to manifest all the godly qualities.

We seldom really know ourselves, much less anyone else. We only see someone's habitual behavior, a product of their life so far. We hold a composite picture of them created from all our memories, memories seen through a judgmental lens. If we haven't liked something they did, we may freeze that moment and put up a little wall to intimacy in that spot in our heart. The reality is that unconditional love can free someone to open parts of themselves that were previously unrealized due to life events.

This is a holy undertaking. Call upon love so that your actions may be in the highest. Speak to your spouse as if speaking to God. In this way your life simply becomes a relationship with God. You might prefer your cultivation of loving-kindness to come from ease, not work, and that will happen. But like all newly activated muscles, efforting is required at the start. Fake it until you make it, or as Thich Nhat Hanh writes, "Sometimes your joy is the source of your smile, but sometimes your smile can be the source of your joy."

In the past you might have complained that changing your behavior for the sake of your spouse was objectionable, too much like manipulation or walking on eggshells. This is different, however, because your actions are not from fear or the purpose of getting your spouse to change. They come from surrendering your will to God's will. (God will take care of your partner's walking.) You are listening to divine guidance and treating your spouse, you might say, impeccably. You will see change, God willing, but not because this is your aim. Divine rewards are inevitable, in the manner and timing of God's choice.

Your spouse will not change in his or her core being. However, in feeling more comfortable and trusting of you, your partner's truer self will begin to emerge from the possibly rough, guarded exterior. Your acceptance of your mate provides a fertile ground for love to flourish. In your gratitude to God for your spouse, you will discover the power and strength of goodness, and miracles will unfold, God willing.

When I check in with God after a conscious interaction with my husband, I can feel God's pleasure. I feel a goodness inside me, not in response to any feedback from my husband, or pride in my efforts, but more like sunshine on a cool day, warming and smiling upon me.

Loving in this way, we can be grateful for our spouse when present but not at a loss when they are absent, because whatever our spouse can or cannot give to us in each moment can be found with God, in abundance, if that is where we set our sights. The only strings we need be attached to are the ones to God.

> *Hold fast unto the bond with God... He has brought your hearts together.*

Objections

As you determine to implement some of these positive changes, you may find it to be more trouble than you anticipated. Objections and complaints will come up. Some of the more prominent ones are addressed in the pages that follow.

The Sun Never Says
Even
After
All this time
The sun never says to the earth,

"You owe me."

Look
What happens
With a love like that—
It lights the whole
World.
—Hafiz

It's Not Fair

You may think, *Why should I be so nice when my spouse is not!*

Because you can. Because it is the right thing to do. Because it pleases God. Be kind so that when you lay your head on the pillow at night you can feel good about your day. Let your spouse be who he or she is, but also remain in expectation of God's generosity. You may soon begin to taste the divinity within you both.

This Is Contrived

Yes, it is contrived, or rather prescribed. It is similar to the adage that if you smile you will be happy. In the process of serving God, and being cautious of your speech, patient in your reactions, speaking only what uplifts, you will be uplifted. You will begin to feel clean and good, and in the process of being loving in your actions, your love and appreciation for your husband *and* yourself will begin to grow.

This Is Too Much Trouble
It's just a game. Is it never-ending?

The greatest mistake you can make in a marriage is to obsess on what you're *not* getting from your spouse. It is so easy to fall back to those thoughts. There are no perfect people. If you can't always be grateful, you can at least do your best to treat your partner with kindness. It is incumbent upon us to be generous of heart.

> *Being grateful brings humility to the heart when it has become all too arrogant, complacent, and insensitive; gratefulness is also the antidote that counteracts our feelings of separation, loneliness and poverty.*

Words Matter
If you are about to speak, take a moment to imagine your words and how they will land on the heart of your spouse. Are they important enough to say even if they are hurtful? Probably not, at least not until you have made a habit of speaking softly and with love.

Soft words soften hearts that are harder than
rock, harsh words harden hearts that are
softer than silk.
—Imam al-Ghazali

Our tone of voice often has a greater impact than the words we say. Speak in a manner that calms and soothes both hearts. Even when agitated, you can learn how to speak with great calm and love, for both your sakes. The effect will be instantaneous.

It was said of one of the prophets that his speech was so measured that you could count his words, each one sending to the person just what they needed to heal their heart or enlighten their mind. Try to parse your words this carefully for a day, or longer. If you adopt this habit on a regular basis, don't be surprised when your beloved begins to listen to you more intensely and more often. (I used to feel like the woman in a *New Yorker* cartoon whose husband says to her, "What have you been saying for the past 40 years, darling?")

They Can Be Like the Sun
They can be like the sun, words.

They can do for the heart
what light can
for a field.
—St. John of the Cross

O God, I take refuge in You from any speech
that creates confusion or results in discord or
sows doubt.

Each word we say matters. Each utterance has
the ability to lift or wound a heart. If you looked
at your regrets in life, words you have spoken and
wished you could take back would be at the top
of the list.

The rule of thumb is this: *Don't complain about*
another's behavior. Be the behavior you want to see.
Don't complain about not being heard. *Listen.* The
more impeccable you become in your communication with others, the more others will respond in
kind.

Every utterance that issues forth does so
with the vestment of the heart from which it
emerged.

When we pause a second before speaking, we
can assess the impact our words will have and
adjust accordingly. Granted, some speech is merely
the transfer of information, but even that provides
an opportunity to supplement the information
with loving-kindness, either by touch or a kind
word. For example, to "Don't forget to feed the
dog," you can add, "Thanks for taking such good
care of him."

It is said that when we speak about someone

else, our words are always carried to their ears—by angels, if there was kindness in them, or by darker spirits if we speak ill. Considering this possibility is a helpful motivator for our desire to eliminate backbiting and to be only generous in our words about others.

A Prayer for You ...

> *Dear Lord,*
> *You are the source of all love, mercy, under-standing and faith. I want to bring greater love to my marriage, but I will need your help. Show me how to be more generous of heart. Increase me in patience. Help me hear your guidance and follow Your way. Make me steadfast in my efforts to nurture love for my spouse, for Your sake. Let me always feel Your presence and support and show my gratitude to You through prayer and right action.*
> *Amen*

Of course, there is no arrival at perfection of love, but hopefully you will begin to notice a lightening of your heart through the adoption of some of the suggestions so far.

Because you and I cannot dialogue, before you move to Part Two, it might be helpful for you to write down your responses to these questions.

- Were there any noticeable positive effects on your relationship as a result of implementing a few of the changes suggested?
- What challenges did you encounter?
- What complaints/stumbling blocks do you still have?

The Divine Quality of Kindness

Sometimes circumstances call for a specific attribute to awaken in our being our best human reflection of one of God's attributes. The quality *Ra'uf,* "the Mild, the Tolerant, the Compassionate, the Kind, the Friendly" is one of those qualities that will help you as you continue on this journey of love. Here is some of what Rosina-Fawzia writes about Ra'uf in her exquisite book on the Divine Names.

> *Ra'uf awakens in our heart a quality of soft-ness, kindness, and friendliness so delicate and permeating that it can resonate through the walls of hatred and malice because we then act from the seat of our true self, in quiet, calm love, instead of reacting from our wounded self where we are upset and hurt. Ra'uf does not help us endure or overcome malice; it eliminates in us every response to it. When Rauf exists, there is nothing to defend, because we are enfolded in the light of kindness which enables us to touch the*

wound in the hearts of others. Because it is out of those wounds that the fears, the over-sensitivity, and the attacks come.

Part Two

6

Tackling the Hard Stuff

You are the way and the wayfarers.
When one of you falls down, he
falls for those behind him, a caution
against the stumbling stone.
Ay, and he falls for those ahead
of him, who though faster and
surer of foot, yet removed not the
stumbling stone.

We all learn from one another, sometimes walking ahead and sometimes holding up the end, with a common goal of coming closer to our divine nature, and to God.

Through our marital conflicts, our particular needs are revealed to us, as well as our fears and doubts, creating the opportunity for us to awaken to the truth: that all the qualities we desire lie within, ready to be brought to light. God can and will provide the totality of what we need.

If your spouse's words and behavior are still troubling, remember this: it is not so much that your spouse *makes* you feel bad about yourself but that in some part of your being, you don't feel good enough to begin with. In making an effort toward conscious unconditional loving, you will begin to feel better about yourself, *inshallah* (God willing), and won't need as much affirmation from others.

There will be things that stand in the way of our efforts to be more loving. Perhaps we don't feel worthy of carrying goodness, our light having been squelched at an early age, so we question our benefit to others. Or we may believe our partner is not worthy of receiving our love. In either case, these illusionary beliefs interfere with our freedom to love and be loved.

The hard truth is that the attitude with which you encounter the world is the attitude you will see reflected back to you. When you are angry, even if you don't acknowledge or act on it, you will encounter anger from others. When you are filled with love, love will come back to you. As you polish the mirror of your heart, the universe will begin to reflect your goodness, and a sense of joy and trust will emerge, in yourself and in God.

We All Carry Wounds from the Past

*When another person makes you suffer, it
is because he suffers deeply within himself,
and his suffering is spilling over. He does not
need punishment; he needs help. That's the
message he is sending.*
—Thich Nhat Hanh

When your spouse does not speak sweetly—or
worse, speaks harshly—look beneath the words.
In that moment, at this juncture in your marriage,
your spouse could not have done other than they
did. Perhaps your mate's heart is really saying,
"I'm scared" or "You don't really care for me."
Your beloved cannot always be the person you
would like them to be because of the nature
of their wounds, just as you cannot always act
from your best self. Your spouse *can* heal, learn,
and outwardly change, but *not* because of your
demands or suggestions, however sweetly veiled.
For significant change to happen, you must change
first: change the eyes through which you see your
beloved, change the words you say or don't say,
and change your relationship to God, the Source
of what you truly need.

Giving love will be easier if you feel nourished
and fulfilled within and not dependent on your

spouse's behavior to validate your self-worth. Build a home for God in your heart from which you can give the clean water of love. Support your efforts through prayer, community, inspirational readings, and spiritual practices. Chapter 8 will address some practices that can nourish and support your walking.

Not My Will but Thy Will Be Done

Every moment provides us with an opportunity to move closer to God or further away. Try to cultivate humility, gratitude, and patience, and avoid lordship, self-management, and arrogance. For if you stubbornly attach to your will, the world may not appear a generous place. In His love and wisdom, God continually presents us with situations that highlight our qualities, both the ones we have polished and the ones that need cleaning; take advantage of these teachings. In our grateful surrender to what *is* lie teachings and secrets beyond the realm of our imagination.

From time to time, we all think that this isn't how our life was supposed to be. We weren't meant to have a wife who nags, a husband who's always angry, a partner who has no spiritual calling. We think we don't deserve this, but in fact we do get what we deserve, or rather what we *need*, in order to help us know more about ourselves. In our mate's anger, we can see our own; in our partner's overspending, we can see our miserliness; in the doubter, our own wavering faith is brought to light. In retrospect, we can see God's wisdom behind all our trials, though not always while we are in the midst of our struggle.

When we do find love, we may end up giving too much or withholding our giving, our natural response being tied to beliefs formed in childhood. We must get unstuck from repeating patterns that do not feed our soul. When we are guarded and insecure, we cannot fully blossom. When our mind makes trouble for our heart, we cannot flourish. The key lies in trust in God and in acceptance of and gratitude for what is.

The gratefulness of the earth manifests when it gives us a surplus of plants, the gratefulness of animals manifests when they give us more than we give them, the gratefulness of plants manifests when they give us generously even when there is little water or the soil is weak, and the gratefulness of the human being manifests through their tongue and their deeds.

Life is full of surprises. God might give one person a very affectionate mate because they are very needy for love. What is being asked of them, then, is that they be grateful, respectful, and reverent in the face of their good fortune, not greedy for more or taking their blessings for granted. On the other hand, God may make it impossible for someone else to get from their spouse the degree of love they think they need, moving them, in their insufficiency, to discover their neediness for God and to open their heart to receive from love's Source.

What about things your mate does that drive you crazy, hurt your heart, or seem just plain wrong? First and foremost, look inside yourself. For each irritation ask yourself why this behavior bothers you so much. Look at your history. Does it spin you back into past events, childhood experiences where you had no control (or freedom, or safety)? Now you seek from others what you did not get as a child, and disappointment will be inevitable. Turn your needs to God, with Whom contentment can be found.

We often attempt to control our environment by trying to create the conditions we once lacked. While we may have some success with this, it puts a burden on us to seek control of that which is inevitably beyond our capability. Efforts to maintain strict control of our surroundings constrains us, spiritually, emotionally, and physically. Struggling to hold on to a life structured to avoid pain takes enormous effort and does not foster love. Our arenas of self-management necessarily exclude divine management, and so create blocks to divine guidance, and we thereby forfeit ease.

Even if your relationship has turned the corner and love abounds, there will still be times when your partner will come out with a harsh word or action that stings your heart. Maybe you will get an apology later but still remain bruised by the event. You would like to let it go, but you can't.

Here is an example of a small event that quickly accelerated into alienation but eventually led to a deep healing. A husband, having some trouble being understood by his wife when he spoke, began to repeat in a booming voice any sentence she queried. He didn't make an effort to get her attention, rephrase the sentence, or speak more clearly but instead, simply repeated the same words *louder*, much like the archetypal tourist in a foreign country. After three days of this, the woman collapsed in despair, feeling separation and self-doubt. She sought help from a friend and healer, and in their session she remembered that when she was a young girl her father, with whom she was very close, would sometimes shout at her impatiently when she asked questions, resulting in her feeling stupid and unloved. This knowledge had been buried in her unconscious for decades. When she made that connection, she released a torrent of tears, followed by great relief, and then a rush of mercy for her father.

She took some time for rest and prayer. Her emotions related to the event with her husband were washed, and only a deep gratitude remained for the understanding that had come with the trial, her gift within the challenge. Later, she was able to share her discovery about her father's impatience and the nature of her sensitivity. She was then able to gently tease him for his behavior, and their laughter established that all antagonism had passed. Also, he paid more attention to his speaking in the future.

When things are going well, we may forget that relationships need tending. Just like plants and animals, human relationships need consistent care, physical and spiritual. After experiencing a nice plateau of peace and goodwill, you may feel a bit of a shock when anger or disrespect comes toward you out of nowhere. The truth is that conflict doesn't come out of nowhere. It is usually a signal that you have been functioning on automatic and have become unconscious of your words and deeds and their effects on others. You have drifted into the comfortable anticipation of eternal bliss as a reward for all of your previous efforts.

What Hit You Could Not Have Missed You

During times when your relationship does not go smoothly, your partner may not be inclined—then or ever—to examine with you what you both might have done differently. If that is the case, the most fruitful communication you can have is with God or a spiritual guide. Allow yourself to feel your grief or anger, with no regrets or apologies for being vulnerable. Be glad for your spouse's apology, if and when it comes, but don't depend on it alone to heal your discomfort.

When we are triggered by our spouse's behavior, a chain of events is set into motion. First our hearts and souls object to the behavior, to varying degrees, sometimes severe. We feel undeserving of such treatment. When our emotional reaction is out of proportion to the offensive behavior, such as rage or despair—when we feel like the rug has been pulled out from under us and our dreams of a loving relationship have been ripped asunder—it is best to get help soon. Courage comes from squarely facing our potent feelings, but there are times we don't want to go there on our own. A spiritual healer whom you can trust can accompany you as you visit the deepest roots of your discomfort.

> *To get what you love, you must first be patient with what you hate.*
> —Imam Al-Ghazali

> *If you see a person behaving poorly, e.g., they are angry and blaming while you are calm and polite, and their behavior makes you "blame and object" to them, then their mistake "becomes visible because of your hardness." Otherwise, how far they had*

strayed might have gone unnoticed by them.
But "if you are ripe in your" best self, and in
a place where you are "obliged to help others,
you will adopt a better way in which you will
remain unchanged within … yet at the same
time you … can erase their mistake by your
kind judgment and your high morals."

Remaining *unchanged within* when we are judgmental about someone's obviously "wrong" behavior is a difficult discipline, but it is the highest to which we can and should aspire.

The more inner work we do, the less attached we will be to the behavior of others. Behaviors I used to demand my husband apologize for (without success) now go barely noticed. And the irony is that now he will come and apologize for something that, to my mind, warranted no apology. Such are the small miracles that come from building an atmosphere of loving-kindness.

In His mercy, God does not show us all our mistakes, as there are slips we might not yet be able to cope with recognizing. It follows, then, that it is not our job to point out to our spouses what God has chosen to conceal from them. Following what you find to be discomforting behavior, after taking time for self-reflection and finding forgiveness for both of you, you may still feel the need to speak about a certain pattern of behavior that is difficult for you to accept. Be gentle and loving as you speak, and *detach from outcome*; this means you will be okay if this pattern never changes but would like your spouse to know that you struggle with the feelings it arouses. If you can cite an example from your childhood of a family member presenting the same behavior and how it affected you then, it helps take the blame off your spouse as the ultimate cause.

As for a stronger approach, it is not fruitful to demand change of another or make threats based on whether or not their behavior changes, unless you are willing to risk everything, including the marriage. There may be a time for this, but if this is not where you are at present, be merciful for the humanity in you both, and move on, for now.

It may be helpful to examine your relationship with your parent who is the same gender as your spouse. Most of us harbor a bit of mistrust and vulnerability regarding our spouse that can be traced back to a parent or caretaker. It took a decade of healing work with my father before I got my last piece (hopefully), which was that within the good times we had, I also had a sense of my role in keeping him out of depression. I had such fond memories of my childhood with him that I hadn't remembered his dark side. Translating this into my relationship with my husband, it made sense that I felt an unnecessary responsibility to keep him from suffering. Realizing this set me free from a pattern of behavior that was needless and constrictive to my growth—and his.

As my own story demonstrates, most of our limiting beliefs can be traced back to a few roots in our childhood, patterns of relating to significant others that formed our general outlook on the world. In order to find peace, safety, self-esteem, or love, we compromised our true self, establishing habitual ways of reacting to events that we unknowingly continue into the present. These unresolved issues, their effects on the body, and ways to heal are addressed in depth in the recent book *God's Way*.

We are all a bit scared of love. We protect our hearts for numerous reasons. It is uncomfortable to admit our neediness. We may fear the hope that love offers, having once had our hopes shattered or felt the heartbreak of unrequited love. We may feel we are owed for past disappointments, and in our resentment do not want to put ourselves out anymore. We may also fear letting others in because they might not like what they see.

A teacher once told me that at each step, in relation to love, you will say, *This is enough, this is all the love I can hold*. Then, after you become comfortable feeling this depth of love, you are ready to open your heart a bit more. Recognize your heart's capacity to carry love, and be tender with it as it stretches with God's help, and your willingness. The scope of love is endless, as vast as the heavens and beyond. No wonder it is as scary as it is wonderful.

A newlywed couple recently shared with me the benefits of some recent explorations of their feelings. Up until their first Christmas as husband and wife, they had pretty much been honeymooners. Now, facing the anxieties of the holiday season, they were seriously motivated to remove any unexplored feelings that stood between them and the abiding love they knew so well. After a rough week of numerous outside stressors, they finally had time alone. Over the course of several days, they bravely reviewed each and every hurt or frustration either of them had felt during the rush of the holidays, *really* listening to one another. They brought up every event in which one or both of them had felt angry or hurt, an activity they had not had time for while it was happening. After exploring each situation as they both saw it, they created an agreed-upon "unified memory" so their memories of each struggle, when they recalled it, now included both their perspectives rather than two distinct, irreconcilable memories.

The key element was their interpretations of each other's actions. When she realized that it was her husband's *interpretation* of her actions that had angered him, she said to him, "I'd be angry too, if I thought you had intended that." That removal of blame soothed his heart, and he felt understood.

And when she explained the impetus behind her action, he could see the love that was there, and she felt understood.

Compassionate listening and the cleansing of images that block love are not just for honeymooners. Our differences may not always be resolved in words, as happened for that couple, but we also build a mutual understanding through our deeds and thoughts. As you begin to love your spouse anew and the bond of marriage strengthens, you both will be more willing to take measures to sustain and protect this newfound connection of love and trust. This is a major step.

Remember, in each moment your choices can either move you closer to or further from love. As you make more loving choices, your spouse will eventually follow suit because of how good it feels to love.

How We Limit Ourselves and Others

We tend to put people (including ourselves) in boxes, in categories, in static illusions not representative of their true being. It is no wonder we are judgmental. Our established picture of our spouse limits our deeper understanding and stifles their self-expression. The beauty and majesty of their unacknowledged qualities remain concealed.

There is nothing wrong. It may seem wrong
if we have a precise picture of what is right,
but if we look without prejudice, nothing is
wrong. We human beings can only ever see
a part of the picture—never the entirety.
All aspects of human life, the social and the
individual, the spiritual and the material
form an indivisible whole and cannot be seen
separately. So exercise discipline, for true
discipline means ... to look at things without
any preconceptions.

We make judgments based on our pictures. We claim to understand the meaning behind our spouse's actions when even our spouse doesn't fully understand their motivations. *He is so mean,* for example. Have you considered the alternative, that your spouse is wounded and striking out because of those wounds? Your mate may derive no joy from losing his temper, even though he may feel justified at the time.

Observe how strongly you hold on to the images of who you are and who your spouse is, and how from that standpoint you decide what your marriage should look like. In our limited understanding, we make our spouses and ourselves small. We must strive to see beyond our images and interpretations and into the endless possibilities for each of us and for our marriage. Growth is messy, full of mistakes. It requires relinquishing control over the evolution of our relationship, and allowing it to flower.

In all likelihood your spouse will continue to be what you anticipate them to be. Yet inside there lies a multitude of possibilities. Look into the eyes of a baby. They have come from the realm of pure spirit. Over time, the shadows of experience will cover over their innate nature to a greater or lesser degree depending on life events, but their essence remains unchanged. It is this divine essence that allows each of our beings to offer whole universes to be explored. Unconditional love can enable both parties to enter those infinite realms.

Know that your relationship can change and *will* change as you do this work. Neither you nor your spouse knows now what lies within, waiting to be awakened. Be in expectation of miracles as you embark upon the journey of activating love.

Here is a beautiful illustration of how the outside changes when we change inside. A recent acquaintance related to me that for nearly a decade her marriage had been less than good. Her husband had been cold and distant, paying little if any attention to her. Her family and even her husband would attest to that description of their relationship at the time. Unhappy with the circumstances of her marriage, she set about establishing a new attitude.

First, she said, she stopped expecting her husband to be a certain way and accepted what was. Then she began to strengthen her spiritual walking. Over the next two years, following each of her five daily prayers, she prayed for what was "in the highest for the relationship, whatever that might be." Then she did an unusual thing. She imagined herself on a pedestal, and her husband praising her, loving her, and admiring her. Every day in her imagination, five times a day during those moments of prayer, she was the delight of her husband's eyes.

What transpired was that slowly his heart became drawn to her, and an amazing thing happened. He turned his heart fully to her, adoring her and giving her his complete love. The change in him was obvious to everyone. He had gone from being withdrawn and cold to being totally loving. He came to adore her, just as she had imagined. He said to her one day, "I could not see you until now. I feel safe in your presence." In their state of newfound love, and having been childless for a very long time, they saw a fertility doctor and now have a beautiful newborn baby girl.

How did this work? God knows. In acknowledging the reality of her imagination, she honored the world of the subtle. She began to feel herself as lovely and desirable. She allowed her husband to be who he was, which created a safe container for him. Most importantly, she remained open to all possibilities, and surrendered to God's will. This was the catalyst for the miracle.

•   •   •

As you develop your own divine qualities, you will begin to notice the same qualities in others. *Your heart will begin to teach you what your mind could not.* Your sight and your hearing will change because your heart is infinitely more capable than your mind of perceiving the brilliance of the ever-changing world of God's creation.

As you continue to follow divine guidance, you may still have to put your foot down on occasion, but you will now feel the strength of God behind your words of truth. *No. This is not right. This feels wrong to me.* Keep it short, be loving, allow the power of God's truth to flow through you like a beam of light, and detach from outcome.

And finally, keep a sense of humor. As John Travolta, playing the mischievous angel in the movie *Michael*, says, "You gotta learn to laugh. It's the way to true love."

7

Successes and
Cautionary Tales

*Do not lose hope in the acceptance of
an act of yours wherein you found
no awareness of the divine Presence.
Sometimes He accepts an act the
fruit of which you have not perceived
right away.*

L ife never fully conforms to our desires and
demands. We must be gentle with ourselves,
allowing past hurts and disappointments to be
acknowledged and released. Though we may need
time to grieve the loss of our idyllic dreams, we

can and will move beyond them to a new way of being. Majesty and beauty always surround us; we have only to change the lens through which we see.

When you aspire to make a home for God in your heart and begin to give of yourself in ways that may not be easy, you will soon feel God's pleasure for your devotion and service. In the act of giving, you will find a deep inner joy. You will feel sufficed. You will come to know that God is always enough.

You might be impatient to get to the part where you can let your spouse know what they are doing wrong. Not yet. First you must befriend your beloved mate. The bonds of trust between you need strengthening. Your spouse must know in their heart how much you love and appreciate them. Then, because your voice will be so healing, your partner will begin to listen to you. Your mate will become like the student's husband who said, "I have never really seen you before." When regularly out of your mouth come words like "My beloved, you must be having a rough day" or "Thank you so much for clearing the dinner table," and the like, they will feel the love behind your words, and you will too. After a while it may feel safe for your mate to open up to you from a deeper place, to perhaps let you in on their mistakes, worries, or triumphs. But this level of intimacy cannot be pushed. It will evolve.

Concerns and Options

After you've had a month or two without serious quarrels, enjoying each other's presence and getting to know one another at a new level, then you can drop in a gem of a concern. You essentially have two choices regarding a behavior of your spouse that you wish would go away.

- First, since the behavior hasn't changed, in spite of your best efforts, you can simply let it be, especially if it is a habitual behavior, like not running the garbage disposal. When you have the urge to remind your beloved that they didn't run it, recognize your impulse to point that out but instead say nothing. Feel good about your restraint and also take a look at why this behavior has been so bothersome to you. It likely goes beyond the particular behavior to similarly frustrating situations in your past.
- Or, if it is a behavior that disturbs you enough of the time, you might — with love in your heart, calmness in your voice, and detachment from outcome — mention a small gem of observation, e.g., "Beloved, you may not know it, but I get depressed when you complain about politics first thing in the morning. When you get angry at whoever is delivering the morning news, I get upset, and want to protect them. That may

sound silly, and I am working on it, but for right now this situation causes me discomfort. I'm not asking you not to listen to the news if that is what you need, but I may think about taking my breakfast on the porch for a few days."

Regarding the second choice, allow a little time the next morning before you pack up your breakfast because the chances are good that your spouse will be quietly reading the news, not vocally arguing with the people on the morning show, at least for now. Why the change? Because you took responsibility for your reaction, made no demands, and were not attached to your spouse changing. You accepted that your partner couldn't have done anything differently at that time, because that's what they have always done in the morning, but you have planted a seed regarding what would please you. When your spouse changes this behavior, it will be by choice, not coercion, and the credit will go to your mate. Everybody wins.

Greater ease develops when you make fewer demands on your spouse and feel more gratitude for this person to whom you are married. When you feel inwardly fulfilled, through whatever spiritual support you find, and are no longer as dependent upon your spouse filling so many of your needs, there is a much greater chance that your mate will be generous. The pressure is off.

Think of having two children, one who is always demanding and one who asks for nothing. Though you may give to both, which one offers you more pleasure in the giving? It will be easier for your spouse to meet your needs when there is freedom of choice.

If you want things to change in any relationship, it helps to let go of the reins of control. Let go of your beliefs about love, let go of your self-importance or insecurity, and let go of your certainty that you know better. Assume you know nothing. Essentially, your ego needs to disassemble so your heart can become your guide.

Sometimes so much is going on in our lives, and we have so many other things to be concerned about, that we can't help being angry that our partner isn't making the same effort to be loving as we are. This is a difficult situation to address. However, feeding the picture that your husband or wife is in the wrong will only increase your anger, resentment, and sense of righteousness. All you can really do when you feel like this is to confess that you have run out of patience and then lie low until the anger passes. Let your spouse know that they are not the cause of your anger (even though they may have been the catalyst and last straw). Having a bad day and admitting it gives both of you the permission to have times when you run out of patience, for whatever reason. Letting your spouse know they weren't at fault reminds *you* of that truth, shows compassion for them, and models permission to be fallible, without blame or guilt.

In short, endeavor to let go of your opinions of what your husband or wife should be doing, or how they should be. Let them make mistakes. Let yourself make mistakes. Let it be, let it go, let God.

It may be appealing to go back to your old ways of reminding your husband or wife of what they could do better, with the intent of changing them—just a wee bit! Things are going well now, and really, they weren't so bad before you started working so hard to be loving. Be cautioned, though, that as soon as you let up on your efforts, you will feel a subtle difference. There will be more separation between your hearts. Your spouse will seem less comfortable. Your partner's trust in your support, love, and respect will lessen. You will be able to restore this trust sooner than the first time you made the effort to do that, but it will be something of an uphill battle to return to the same level of intimacy and love. There will be a delay between when your gentle self resurfaces and your spouse responds and relaxes. Remember, it is love you both seek—that is the magic behind your new creation, the glue that keeps you together. Love is a devotion that continuously rewards, so return to love, time and time again.

It is vital to resist the temptation to tell your husband or wife just how hard you have been working to be loving. It will destroy the mystery and reduce them to the object of an experiment. This is between you and God. Don't let on that learning loving-kindness has been a project of yours. We all think we deserve to be loved, so it will just seem natural to your spouse when you shower appreciation on them. As you continue to be more loving, your spouse will begin to be more loving too. It's only natural.

Examples

Here is an example from my own experience of turning from blame to love. I was coming home one day from a walk around the neighborhood, feeling perfectly fine, or so I thought. I passed by a man washing his car, playing the most heavenly music, and I instantly burst into tears. The music was so tender, the man so kind (stopping to look up the singer's name for me), and the contrast to my daily life so great that I wept for what I was missing. My immediate thought was *Why isn't my husband that tender and kind to me?* My resentment began to take hold, until I quickly realized the dangers of ruminating on what I *don't* get from my husband. While I finished my walk, I invited God to show me tender mercy (in Arabic, *Latif*), that I might feel it in my heart, and know it, and *become it* with His help. I entered my home in the rarified state of having experienced *real* and *expansive* tenderness inside and wanting and praying to know it better. As I sat alone with that quality, I began to understand that tender mercy is always available if we seek it but that, metaphorically, I had been stomping on it, scattering the tender mercy like our cats scatter in a room when I enter in haste. I perceived it emanating from the baseboards of every room, spilling out across the floor, filling the room with divine tender mercy—if only I could be quiet enough, gentle enough, subtle enough to not disturb it.

Later, when I came down to fix dinner, I was still experiencing the sweetness of tender mercy. My walking, my speech, and my touch were quiet and soft, without effort. When my husband turned to me, he spoke more gently than usual, and held my gaze for longer. I realized that I was transmitting that quality of mercy.

> *Tenderly I now touch all things,*
> *knowing one day we will part.*
> —St. John of the Cross

When I was immersed in that subtle place, I was responded to in kind. This is what I mean when I say that when *we* change, our environment changes. As we more fully carry any quality—love, mercy, peace, or kindness, for example—others will reflect back to us the same, to some degree. They become enveloped in the light we carry, and it ignites a similar light inside them. You could use the analogy of tuning forks. When we ourselves tune to a higher frequency, that resonance vibrates within the other as well.

Here is story that highlights how what we witness on the outside is influenced by what we carry on the inside. I had some sessions with a young woman who had a generous heart but was unhappy. She came to me because she was scared. Her annual mammogram had revealed a cyst with a small dark spot that was of concern to her doctor. Even before the first session was over, she recognized that she had closed off her heart to her family. The precipitating factor was her frustration with the fact that she and her husband had lived with his parents for over a decade. Her unmet need to move into a home of their own was causing her much grief. Not wanting to feel this deep frustration and unhappiness, she admitted that she had closed off her heart for protection. Compounding her desolation was the fact that her older sister had died several months earlier.

After one session together, because of her sincerity and goodness, she was able to quickly grasp the situation and realize that she was the one who needed to change. She determined to open her heart then and there. Shortly after our session, she was on the phone with a close friend, crying over her sister's death, when her mother-in-law quietly slipped into her room and simply handed her a glass of water and left. This was an extraordinary event in their household.

The day before, the young woman had vowed to open her heart to her mother-in-law but hadn't known how to approach her. Yet even in the *thinking* of opening her heart, her mother-in-law was drawn to do something she would never have done before. When the call was over, the young lady went to her mother-in-law's room and they both cried and shared their unstated love for one another, love that had been blocked for a very long time.

Everything in the household was changing, the woman told me in a later session. For example, she described how previously when she went into the kitchen for breakfast and her in-laws were there, she would feel uncomfortable and leave as soon as possible. Now when she goes into the kitchen, she is glad to see them and they appear happy to see her. Moreover, she shared, her in-laws seem more comfortable with one another and have begun to spend more time together. In short, when the woman opened her heart, the love in the house began to flow.

She reopened her heart not only to her mother-in-law but also to her husband. The young woman was able to honestly say to her husband, "I'm okay staying here. My heart is at peace." A month later, in even deeper acceptance of her situation, she shared the rediscovered truth that her real home was in his heart, and an ease settled between them.

This is a tale of how a change of heart and an acceptance of her situation transformed a woman's life and the lives of those around her. Even the woman's mother, who did not live with them, remarked that her daughter's whole face and demeanor had changed, and she inquired of me as to what her daughter had done.

What *had* the young woman done? She realized her heart was closed. She sought God's help to open her heart. When her heart opened, everyone in her close circle felt safe to do the same — miraculous and yet so simple. *And* when the woman went back to the doctor for her biopsy, he could no longer find the dark spot in her breast and told her a biopsy would no longer be needed.

All of this change came about from a medical scare and her response of seeking spiritual help. Her deep faith and good nature enabled her to open her heart easily, once she recognized that it had been closed. She strengthened her relationship to God for continued support. She began to listen to her own feelings and needs and to care for herself more tenderly, *and* she accepted her situation for the time being. This is a prime example of receiving an uncomfortable nudge from God and seeing the opportunity for growth within the challenge.

Cautions to Consider

There are two cautions to watch for as things begin to improve. One is putting your husband or wife before God to the detriment of your spiritual growth. You can start to overdo your loving deeds toward your spouse, acting less out of love and more out of fear of losing your newfound love connection. In forgetting the Source of your love, you can fall from a state of gratitude into a state of apprehension. This fear comes when you move into acting from self rather than acting to please God because human love is necessarily limited and has strings attached, whereas giving love unconditionally connects you to the unlimited source of God's love.

The second caution is that when things go well you can slip back into your old unconscious ways and forget to regard the relationship as precious. *Reverence for love is key.* As with gardens, love must be tended to regularly and consciously. Of course, there will be days—we all have them—when everyone irritates you and nothing pleases you. However, going down the road of thoughts like *Oh, if my husband were just like this or that, or if he would just do this or that, my life would be easier* only make matters worse. These thoughts can quickly take you from love to dislike. It is never about the other person. It is *always* about you.

We must learn to recognize the subtle signs

indicating that we have stopped giving from the overflow and begun to give from self. Being dutiful from the place of should, not from your heart's desire, will lead to resentment, and the renewed trust between you two will begin to crumble. This is the time to pull back, not in anger but in retreat, so you can find what you need inside through spiritual practices and other activities that return you to a place of peace.

Marriage is not a static structure but rather an ever-changing dynamic. Your spouse is still the same person in their essence, although your unconditional love has brought out the best in you both. If you return to your unconscious self, your mate will too. When you go back to seeing your beloved's faults, not their godly essence, you risk returning to an irritated self- righteousness, telling yourself that you deserve better.

The change starts with your letting your partner know what he or she has done that is causing you difficulty, which causes them to pull back from you. When your spouse becomes more distant, you become even more dissatisfied and may start to become pushier about your needs, from insecurity or fear of separation. There are certain common patterns of discord that can, through their recognition, be avoided. Chapter 9 holds some of the mysteries behind these dynamics, learned from ancient Sufi teachings.

The Divine Quality of Tenderness

Latif is the subtle, the tender, the gently all-pervading ... Latif means gentleness toward all creatures. Its tender kindness works in the background. So be gentle to all creatures, and when you call them, do so with softness and tenderness in your heart....

Latif is a softening energy of love that helps us relinquish that which is coarse and turn to that which is delicate and subtle in us, not out of weakness but in order to move closer to our true self.... The subtle love energy of Latif comes from the heart and conquers the mind. Our understanding is given a more delicate, contemplative quality, and this, in turn, influences our deeds ... Latif refines the veils of our ego that lie on our heart, so much so that the divine light shines through in us.

Dear God, whose tender kindness to His creatures is all prevailing, and Whose goodness reaches His every worshipper, do not remove us from the circle of tender mercy, and secure us from all we fear ...

O God, Your tender mercy is Your protection and Your protection is our tender mercy at any time. So admit us into the tents of Your tender mercy and pitch for us the pavilions of Your protection.

Accompany me with Your tender gentle-
ness, O Tender One. Be near me.
   O Tender One. O Subtle One. O Kind
One. We beseech Your tender mercy forever.
Amen

Part Three

8

Review and Supportive Practices

*He knew you would not accept mere
counsel, so He made you sample the
world's taste to a degree that separation from it would be easy for you.*

To summarize the teachings so far and preview
the chapters to come, I offer these suggestions
regarding your relationship with your spouse:

- Overlook "wrong" behavior (excluding physical abuse, drug use, or a high or constant level
of verbal abuse).

- Minimize judgment.
- Accept self-responsibility; resist blame.
- Adopt speech that uplifts.
- Model loving-kindness in thoughts, words, and actions, without expectation of return.
- Do unto your partner as God would have you do.
- Establish the support of spiritual practices, self-care, and community.
- Open to receive the divine love that is always available.
- Observe how love grows as you share it with others.
- Remember to be in gratitude.

These actions may not be easy or achievable all the time, but they are goals to set your sight upon. You may find yourself quite vulnerable when you first increase your efforts to be more loving. It is natural to feel more sensitive and needy as you strive to give kindness without expecting the same in return. It is important to protect your tender self, this inner treasure of generosity and love you are unveiling. In order to maintain your aspirations, additional support now becomes crucial, to both strengthen and reward your good intentions.

Spiritual Community

Finding spiritual community is not difficult in this age of computers, if you know what you are seeking. Some form of community is advantageous to support your spiritual growth. My path is Sufism, so the University of Sufism, the Farm of Peace, and the Institute of Spiritual Healing come to mind as places I could suggest that offer programs through Zoom and in person. Identify your own needs, though, and search accordingly. Even if your first attempts don't pan out, by the process of elimination you will draw closer to knowing what feeds your heart, and you may also meet some fellow travelers along the way.

Spiritual Practices

> *The path is love, and love is nourished through spiritual practices and sincerity, until the heart and the spirit understand the meaning of existence.*

> *For everything there is a polish, and the polish of the heart is the remembrance of God.*

For complete fulfillment, it is only in your godly connection that you'll find real and eternal companionship. *God is closer to you than your jugular vein*. It is important to establish regular practices that connect you to this Source of love so you can continually refill your heart's supply of loving-kindness.

> *Sometimes lights come upon you*
> *And find the heart stuffed with the forms of*
> *created things,*
> *So they go back from whence they descended.*

To allow the godly light to find a home in us, spiritual practices are essential. Consistent practices are said to be more beneficial than spurts of intense activity, so creating a schedule will be helpful. Early morning, late evening, and night-time are times we are generally more receptive to practices such as prayer, meditation, or chanting. Another way to maintain your godly connection is through listening to or reading spiritual works and teachings, whether in a group or alone. It takes time to find the practices that best support you, and time to experience the subtle results of new or lengthened practices.

Our rational mind may talk us out of spending more time in prayer, study, meditation, or recitation, making us doubt that these endeavors actually do anything. But if we persist and patiently trust the process, we will begin to experience the effects of these practices on our hearts and bodies.

Although we think we want to be free to do whatever we want, whenever we want, real freedom is always found within some element of structure. Maintain your daily practices until your body and soul can't imagine a day without them.

Everything we do is a spiritual practice if done with reverence. For example, if you love cooking, and feed others wholesome food made with love, that is a holy endeavor. Your devotion to bringing more love into your marriage is a spiritual practice. It is the intent behind our actions, not the actions themselves, that imbues them with holiness.

Actions are lifeless forms,
But the presence of an inner reality of
sincerity within them
Is what endows them with life-giving Spirit.

The *sincerity* of your intentions gives a boost to whatever practices you undertake. If you lose sincerity in what you say or do, take some time for self-care until your passion returns. An indication that you need a short break is the loss of peace, joy, or gratitude. That is when you owe it to yourself to take a vacation from tending to others and instead tend to yourself until you are replenished. In the future, note that keeping a balance between serving others and caring for yourself supports consistency in your commitment to love.

Supporting Practices

There are certain practices common to all religions, suggesting their universal value. Among these are ritual prayer, personal prayer, contemplative prayer, rites of repentance, and songs of praise.

Personal Prayer, or Du'a

Sometimes prayers descend upon us unbidden, as when we are overwhelmed with love for God, such as The Garden Du'a, in Appendix B. At other times our du'a are simply conversations with God. Du'as of supplication, detailed below, are another wonderfully fulfilling practice to strengthen and enrich our intimate communication with God.

> *When He loosens your tongue with a request, then know that He wants to give you something.*

Ask for What You Need

It is okay to ask God for what you need. Beseeching God is an acknowledgement that He is the only source of help. It is a practice some of us may not have grown up with, so it can feel a bit clumsy at first. But as you converse, speaking your thoughts openly and respectfully, your heart will become engaged and your deeper needs will be revealed; you will find the reverence that comes from entering into a sacred intimacy with your Lord.

Here is a suggested format if you are just beginning to explore prayers of supplication.

Beginning: Address God with reverence.
Dear God, the One upon Whom I rely, the Source of all understanding (peace, patience, truth, healing, love, faith, holiness, etc.)

Middle:
Suggested openers:
Beloved God,
Protect me from ...
Help me surrender my ...
I take refuge in You from ...
Fill my Being with ...
Let me not forget ...
Teach me ...
Help me ...
Clear for me ...
Keep me ...
Grant me ...
I am grateful for ...
I ask You for ...
Dispel from me ...
Purify me that I may ...
Free me from ...
Forgive me ...

Closing: Prayers of gratitude, blessings and praise, for example:

Thank You, dear Lord, for listening to my prayers and for opening my hearing to Your response. Increase me in faith that my prayer will be answered, in the manner and time of Your choosing.

Peace be upon the prophets and saints, and praise be to God.

Amen

The Divine Quality of the One Who Answers Prayers

Mujib is a helpful quality to remember when praying. *Mujib* is the One Who answers prayers and fulfills them, because "when you turn to Him, it means that you believe in Him and hope to be heard ..." It is not only about our asking, but also about listening, because "praying to God means to invite the divine light into the dark ... so that we may be surrounded by light and come to know what we are actually requesting. In this way we also begin to see the answers that are always there. It is this asking and praying that make us into that which we must become, that opens us to the Divine. Hearing and answering must be attuned." When we open our heart, "request and answer meet.... To know that the answer will come makes lovers out of us."

9

Sufi Secrets

This chapter offers an innovative approach to heal discord in marriage, addressed specifically to women, although one could interpret the suggestions as ways to carry the quality of the feminine, because each of us, regardless of gender, is on occasion called upon to be mother, sister, daughter, or wife to a loved one.

Because the essences of women reflect the ideal of God and give rise to what truly is, if she surrenders to the man he has the chance to witness the divine.

Appropriately, the Arabic words for compassion and mercy, *Rahman* and *Rahim*, come from the same root as the word for womb, *rahima*. The opening quote is saying that women reflect the ideals of God, compassion, and mercy, and that if the woman gives her purest love to her husband, he will taste divinity through her presence.

The woman is not made less by her surrender to the man; rather, she is establishing herself in the place of holiness that is her true nature. Her real surrender is to the One. This surrender is not the same as accepting behavior that is not right, such as hostility or negligence. It is a surrender to God and to the committed relationship—the union of the two—that results in the eventual dissolution of both egos. The woman bows from the truth of her being to the truth of his being. She commits to the cleansing of her being by facing and walking through marital challenges into the teachings that are hidden within them. She maintains the practices and actions that bring her closer to her divine nature while placing her husband's walking in God's hands.

Sufi Mystical Teachings on Men and Women

Through love, we dissolve in order to become love. For men, the path of transformation goes

through self-knowledge, for women through
self-love.

Or you could say this: women love themselves
through loving, and men understand themselves
through the woman's love.

It is wondrous how my interpretation and
implementation of some of the mystical teachings regarding the male and female in sacred
relationship completely explained the nature of
the continual quarrels between my husband and
myself. Once the understanding was there, the
tools for healing became self-evident.

In biblical or, if you wish, metaphorical terms,
when the spirit of Eve is taken from the essence of
Adam, the empty space in Adam is filled with yearning for her, which is really his yearning for his own
wholeness. "Therefore, Adam bends toward Eve
just as he bends toward his own self, because she
is a part of him. Eve bends toward Adam because
he is the homeland from which she came." In a
sense, "the man does not complete himself without
the woman, nor does the woman complete herself
without the man. This is so that together they can
arrive at the witnessing of God. This is the difference
between the love of the spirit and the love of the
body in an intimate relationship. His yearning for
her is his yearning for himself, and her yearning
for him is her yearning to return home."

Practically stated, the man's desire for the

woman is his yearning to understand himself, through her mirror, and her desire for him is her yearning to come home: to his physical arms, yes, but also to her wholeness. Hence for man, the desire for union is the seeking of the whole for its part and for woman, the part for its whole.

If I may generalize from these teachings and my own observations, women, or the carriers of the feminine in a relationship, need the surety and safety of a home base in the arms and hearts of their husbands so they can be the carriers of love, forgiveness, peace, and wisdom that are their inheritance. Men, or the carriers of the masculine,* need to feel loved and safe from criticism in their homes in order to step into their true nature and step out into the world with confidence and strength.

These writings suggest that the wife plays a major factor in how her husband sees himself, while the husband is vitally important to her as a safe place of rest and grounding.**

The interpretation, in summary:

- The man wants to fully understand who he is, and the woman can help enormously through

---

*   I realize these roles can change as well, but for the general meaning of this teaching, I will return to speaking of husbands and wives.

**   These teachings may help any couple, regardless of gender, but I can only reflect from my experience.

the manner in which she reflects *to* him what she perceives *in* him. Whatever godly quality she mirrors back for him—e.g. goodness, or steadfastness, or competence—enables him to see that in himself, and he is content.

- The woman wants to return to a home base of peace, safety, and love. When he can *be* that home for her heart, she is content.
- Her finding comfort in him makes the statement that *who he is inside* is good enough, and he feels complete.
- His provision of a place of rest for her, no questions asked, suffices her, and she feels complete.

Application

How does this operate in day-to-day living, and how would it look if you shifted every interaction with your husband based on these ancient mystical teachings?

The first step to understanding is to observe the nature of your disagreements. There are usually common themes, repeating patterns, to your moments of discord. There will be certain things that trigger you and certain things that trigger your husband. Of course when both of you react strongly at the same time, conflict is inevitable. The solution for preventing future conflict may lie in the application of the mystical teachings that opened this chapter.

Let's look at two scenarios:

- He hurts your feelings with harsh words. When you let him know your heart is hurting, he gets angry at you. Neither of you understands why he gets mad or withdraws from you when you are the one needing commiseration, but it happens repeatedly because somewhere inside he believes he has failed.
- On the other hand, maybe you are having a rough day and you snap at him. He then gets angry and/or withdraws, unable or unwilling to empathize with your stressed self. Even if you later apologize for having been short tempered, he cannot fully take it in. In fact, he may become angry at you, as it brings up the whole event again, an experience that contained the underlying expectation that he should have been more helpful.

As you look at these two sample disagreements, observe the common pattern:

1. Regardless of who got angry first, the man ends up feeling less than, so he emotionally withdraws for protection. He needs to feel good about himself, but the sequence of events mirrored only his failure: in the first, that he hurt you, and in the second, that he could be of no help. He retreats into himself.

2. The woman is hurt and disappointed by the man's anger and/or emotional withdrawal. In the first instance, she is confused and hurt by his anger and lack of apology; in the second she is hurt because he did not commiserate with her hard day, or accept her apology. In fact, her apology only made matters worse. She feels the agony of separation and needs to connect, but he is no longer available.

3. The couple separates physically and emotionally, not fully understanding what happened and not easily able to make it right again.

Either party could reverse this, but in my experience, the woman holds the key and therefore needs to take the first step. Even her actions alone can completely shift the dynamics of the relationship.

Note, if you are a man reading this chapter, I'm not suggesting that you tell your wife what she should be doing, but rather I suggest that you take the lead. Make her always welcome in your arms and in your heart, through your words and deeds, as discussed in previous chapters. This recognition of safety with you will lead to her heart responding with a greater outpouring of love.

To both partners, in short, if you wish to halt discord when it starts, these steps will help:

- The wife gives a positive, intimate reflection back to her spouse, even if unrelated to the topic of the quarrel.
- The husband makes an effort not to run off, close up, or get angry but rather to stay present to his spouse until the discomfort passes.

Another viewpoint is that it is not so much *you* the man loves, but that in loving you he feels good about himself. When he is not comfortable with what you said or did, he loses the feeling of love and feels bad inside. In truth, he is angry at *himself*, not you. Offer him an opportunity to show he cares: some physical gesture, like a hug or helping with some task. Yes, there will be time later for addressing your hurt feelings, particularly when you become clearer about their nature. Although his action hurt you, the place of hurt was already there.

How you can help: how you communicate with your husband through your thoughts, words, and actions will be vitally important. Let's look at your current efforts, related to:

- Listening
- Speaking
- Refraining from speaking
- Thinking
- Touch

*Listen to what is said and follow what is
best in it.*

First, *listen* to your spouse. The most effective
way to show compassion to another is to listen to
what is said and follow what is best in it. Sometimes
that is all they need. Next, speak kindly to your
spouse and never speak ill of him to others, even
just to relate some action you didn't like. Nothing
good will come of it. If you must, then speak to
someone who will turn the issue back on you for
your healing. Be vigilant even of your thoughts,
for a negative perception never goes unnoticed,
however subtle; negative thoughts about the other
can powerfully weaken your relationship. Lastly,
be aware of the healing power of touch, and its
numerous ways and opportunities to highlight
connection and dispel feelings of separation.

An Example of Efforts to
Change a Partner's Behavior

Consider what bothers you most about your husband. Maybe you want him to really listen to you,
compliment you, say he loves you, or be more
supportive, in word and deed. Both husbands and
wives usually have some small grievance they
would change if they could. The example below
is about a wife wanting her husband to listen to
her, but it could just as well be any other request
or suggestion to him to change his behavior.

Here is a sample dialogue *over a year's time* of a wife hoping to be listened to and trying every possible approach with her husband. Although on the surface the tale may seem a bit humorous, it is more likely frustrating and sad because her persistence creates separation between the two of them by focusing so much attention on what her husband is doing wrong. The exchange will eventually weigh heavily on them both. Here is the progression of her efforts:

- *You never listen to me!* (By which she infers he doesn't care about her.)
- *It hurts my heart when you don't look at me when I'm talking.* (She appeals to his empathy.)
- Then, sweetly spoken, *I need to feel valued, and when you don't listen to me, I feel sad.* (Now, owning her part, she asks for his help.)
- *Beloved, I cherish our marriage. It is a sacred bond. It is important that we respect and listen to one another.* (Invoking a higher need.)
- Then, wanting to compromise, *Would you please just acknowledge that you have heard me when I speak?*
- Finally, *Maybe you could say some word, like uh huh, or give me eye contact, after I have spoken, indicating you have heard me.* (A practical accommodation that incurs intermittent change.)
- Finally, gently, *Say yes if you heard what I just said.* (This places the onus on the woman, so it works if she wants to use it.)

Don't you think the man would change if he could? Do you assume from his response that he doesn't love his wife?

In light of our teachings, you might predict that even the gentlest suggestions for how and why your husband should change a habitual behavior seldom result in any lasting change. This is because no matter how sweetly you point out to him what he could and should do better, you actually crush his heart a bit, or even evoke anger, although he may not show it or even know it. In effect, a part of you is saying, "You are not the person I want you to be." Hearing your request, which he cannot meet, he starts to feel his insufficiency, and for protection he pulls back (or if angry, acts out). In that state he is not able to tend to your needs. Your disappointment in his reaction is great, and it shows, making him feel worse. You'd think he'd want to change for you, but he seems to do just the opposite. He retreats even further; you feel uncared for and resentful, and he feels annoyed and crummy.

It doesn't matter which of several behaviors you hope to eradicate; the pattern is the same.

What happens is this:

- You essentially show your husband what's wrong with him, and his image of himself becomes diminished.

- From that place he cannot easily feel or give love.
- He withdraws or gets angry.
- You lose your safe place in his heart, which is your deepest need.
- The relationship suffers.

Emotional separation can happen in the blink of an eye yet take much longer to repair. If your target is to strengthen love and trust, then let little things go for a while. If you really think you don't bring up your spouse's mistakes, then try to go through a day without redirecting his behavior. It may be more of a challenge than you think.

Words Matter

They can be like a sun, words.
They can do for the heart what light can
for a field.

It is written in the holy books that creation is set into motion with *the word*. In the Old Testament, *And God said, Let there be light, and there was light.* In the Qur'an, *He but says unto a thing be—and it is, kun faya kun.* Your words also set into motion the light of a new creation as you speak. The moments we most regret are most often when we have said words that we wish we could take back. Words can heal or destroy.

Because your husband loves you and you are his spouse, *you* are the main source for his deep knowing about himself, though he may be only subtly aware of this. It is an uncomfortable position for him to be in, beholden in that way. It doesn't matter how arrogant or competent you may believe him to be—inside there is still a tender place.

Therefore, *genuinely reflecting back to your husband small observations of appreciation can be very healing.* Through your acknowledgment of his positive qualities, he is able to see and appreciate those qualities in himself. As he begins to see himself positively through your eyes, he will more readily step into his godly self.

*Those who forgive others and cover over their
faults so that one can see them enter this
kindness and their faults too are forgiven.*

We are all holy beings doing the best that we can in our humanity. In every dialogue with your husband, you always have a choice whether to speak words that mirror back to him his best self or ones showing him where he has let you down. Why would you continue to remind him where he falls short, when it only makes separation between your hearts? What does it cost you to show your mate his best self? More to the point, what does it cost you both when you hold up a mirror to his frailties?

It is not only about what you say but also about what you don't say. Not only are we trying to speak more pleasantly but it will also be helpful to withhold critical speech, however minimal, at least until greater trust between you is established. Even something simple like "Honey, you left the fridge open" isn't really necessary. Just shut the door yourself. I'm not saying a woman's suggestions, sometimes negatively referred to as nagging, aren't helpful—for example, getting their mate to the doctor or suggesting some dietary changes—but for now let go of the need to remind or suggest. It isn't as necessary as you might think.

Thoughts Matter

Next, look at your thoughts. Remember the lady who imagined her husband putting her on a pedestal until he did? That was not necessarily her aim, but she was tired of her negative thinking about him and the marriage so she changed her image of their marriage and as a result, so did he. Remember, also, the woman who opened her heart to her mother-in-law and how the mother-in-law responded even before the woman's words of love were spoken. The truth is that even our thoughts have the power to hurt or heal.

The quickest way to create antagonism in a marital relationship is to hold negative images about your spouse; we are all so much more than the sum of our actions. Making a pessimistic picture of our spouse's behavior is easily done if we are unhappy, and there is no easy way back once it becomes habitual. For this reason it is important to be vigilant in observing negative thoughts about others *or* yourself, and to curb them in their infancy. Letting go of judgement will allow your husband to open to new ways of being in the safety of your patient and tender mercy.

Love Matters

It helps to believe in the power of love to change a relationship. It helps to be merciful with *ourselves* when we tire or stumble in our attempts to be more loving. The level of mercy described as *Ra'uf*, the Tolerant, is something to aspire to. It is much like the previous description of being "unchanged within" from chapter 6. Our aspiration is to not be rattled by others' behaviors but rather to embody the abiding love and forgiveness of which our hearts are capable.

Touch Matters

Finally, there is touch to consider. You don't have to love everything about him in order to start giving love to your husband. If you are not getting along too well, you both might feel a bit prickly regarding touch, not sure how it will be received. At first he may not trust your touch or kind word, and that's okay. Simply begin with a light touch in passing, e.g. while he is at the computer, when he's done something you appreciate, or just because you are feeling good, even if you don't really feel like touching him.

After a while you will be drawn to linger longer with your casual touch, because we all appreciate touch. For example, at the beginning you might put your hand on his back in passing. As it gets easier and more pleasurable, maybe you rub his shoulders as well, or go a bit out of your way to give a lingering touch. He will come to appreciate your touch because he trusts your intentions. You are no longer holding up the mirror of his insufficiency and so he is beginning to enjoy your presence more. You are slowly building a safe and loving atmosphere. It will feel natural to move into brief and then longer hugs, hugs that meet the needs of you both: yours, to be held and his, to please you.

I repeat my caution to resist the temptation to tell your spouse, "Hey, I'm trying really hard here to be nice." The benefits of our good deeds are lessened when we expect something in return. Be patient and merciful with you both. You will be rewarded for your efforts in a multitude of subtle ways, but not because your spouse owes you.

As you begin to feel God's appreciation, you

will feel better about yourself. When you feel good about yourself, you will find more joy in giving. As you openly appreciate your husband, your love for him will grow and your light will spread to others. It helps to be rich if you are going to be generous.

When love's voice beckons to you, follow him
Though his voice may shatter your dreams
As the north wind lays waste the garden ...
Even as he is for your growth so is he for your
pruning.

I'm not saying to simply see the good and overlook the "bad" in your husband. It goes much deeper than that. It is to find endearing all the complexities and polarities in your mate, to embrace both the wheat and the chaff. To not love the whole package is to miss out on the depth of love that is possible.

Levels of Love

We relate to one another on many levels simultaneously, as our desires are of varying depths. On the material level, food, sex, admiration, success, and power are among the most ego-centered of our wants, and often the most prominent. Our body has nutritional needs that if not met may hinder our spiritual development. The second and less overt level of needs is the level of the heart. We want and need love, peace, empathy, compassion, and safety for our emotional well-being. Our awareness of the next and more hidden levels begins to touch more closely into our relationship with God. These are the levels of the soul, and even deeper, the spirit.

These subtle realms are where we may receive guidance that does not come directly from our mind but from a place of inner knowing. These realms are also the location of the roots of our deepest hurts and deepest longings. It is worth noting that sometimes we are presented with someone who appears to be our "soul mate" but we are not yet able to smoothly navigate the needs of our separate egos and hearts. These teachings of how to practice love at a deeper level may prove helpful in overcoming those obstacles to a loving relationship.

Here is an example of a woman discovering her needs at a deeper level than ego or heart, a depth at which truth became more certain. Remember the woman living with her in-laws? She had recognized her resentment and opened her heart to them and to her husband, which resulted in a noticeable increase in peace and love for everyone. She eventually recognized and acknowledged that her true home was in his heart. Her heart felt clean and nourished, and things went well for some time. Then circumstances changed and her yearning resurfaced, this time from a deeper place.

When her in-laws took a week's vacation, she

and her husband and two children had the rare opportunity of being together, just the four of them. During this time, the peace and love in the house were overwhelming. She realized with great clarity the truth that with their current arrangement, she could not give fully to her husband all the love she had in her heart due to their lack of privacy. Nor could she parent her children as her heart dictated because most of the discipline and guidance were deferred to the grandparents. These needs came from her heart, but the intensity and depth of absolute truth she felt was anchored in an even deeper place.

Now, after the passage of some time, she again felt a yearning to move—but for different reasons and from a different place in her being, a layer in which an expansive love for her husband and her children was crying to be released, a place in which the truth of her being could be honored and could flourish. She had a clarity of guidance and a knowing she had not tasted before.

What was different this time? It was the feeling of holiness and truth at the core of her being. It was as if she was enveloped by a towering light, grounding her in certainty and stretching her to the heavens. She was drawn to gently speak her needs to her husband without demands or attachment to outcome. She simply said, *I am bursting with love for you. It hurts me to hold it back as I must do because we are seldom alone, just the two of us.* She put her hand on her breast where the dark spot had been and told him she worried for her health if she could not give this love that was crying to be released. *You must have noticed how wonderful our relationship was when we were alone,* she said. With courage and grace she spoke her truth, and left the rest to him. After a decade of attempts on her part to be heard, this time, soon after she spoke her truth with love and detachment, he began to initiate plans for their moving into a home of their own.

A Prayer for You ...

Dear Lord, please help us give to others as you would have us do. Help us step beyond our selfish and stubborn desires to that place where your loving kindness can flow through us, and truth and wisdom can follow. Guide us to that place of gentleness and knowing that allows us to be among your leaders of goodness and caring.
Amen

10

The Harvest

They [your wives] are your garment
and you are a garment for them.

Men and women are garments for one another.
He is your garment, and you are his. Clothe
him in the raiment of respect and love, tenderness,
and appreciation. Make the effort to be kinder and
more loving, not out of fear, or to get something in
return, but because it is the right thing to do. Treat
your husband consistently with loving-kindness
and be in wonderment of what ensues for you both.

We can become witnesses to miracles. To see

the massive difference that unconditional love can make, and to be a part of that, is to glimpse the power and holiness of the Divine. Your husband will see *in your eyes* that he is okay down to the depths of his being. This is worth a lifetime of being right.

This adventure of nurturing love, which may have begun from a sense of aloneness, will continue to feed a deeper embodiment of love in every aspect of your life, *inshallah*. When you turn to God for your sustenance and are saturated with divine light, your spouse will want to be near you, to drink from the same intoxicating love. This love will overflow into other relationships as well, and you, too, will feel loved and lovable.

Life with, by, and in God is so rich and expansive that you can actually touch upon the infinite, the eternal. Miracles can happen; aspects of life you never hoped were possible become the norm, when love guides your actions.

Everything comes in God's time. You may have been doubtful, saying to yourself, *I'm too old to change!* You may have felt regret: *Why did I not discover this truth when I was younger?* The path to God is unique for each of us. Some of us were meant to blossom late in life; we had much work to do on ourselves first, and had to make many mistakes to guide us to the right path. The passage of time is not metronomic. In the slipstream of God, in the perfection of each moment, there is no time, and there is no lack, and you may actually taste the sweetness of patience.

You may be noticing by now that the more you actively love your husband, the more love you seem to have for him, as if the source is endless. It is. In addition, the more love you give, the more you begin to receive, in unexpected ways. The forgiveness and mercy you hold for both of you moistens the earth of your marriage for the seeds of abiding love to grow. Your husband will never change his essential being—no one does—but he will begin to be his best self if you start the process by acting from your best self.

The change in your husband will be subtle at first, but through his witnessing your steadfast acceptance and appreciation of him, he will begin to take risks, revealing more of the mysteries of his being. He may not say aloud, "I appreciate what you are doing." He may not even be conscious of the change, but your kindness with no strings attached will loosen his restraint and open the door to intimacy.

Suppose your spouse says something that appears unkind, and you let it go. Perhaps you slip away, not in anger but in acceptance of that part of him. Your grace did not go unnoticed. He may even apologize later, when you do not seek it and least expect it. Through his words, you will witness your Lord's gratitude for you. This is God's mercy at work.

There will be times when you seek his company and times when you want to be alone. Your use of time may have previously been a major source of disagreement. If your husband was usually covetous of the amount of time you spent apart from him, expect this to lessen. By the same token, if he usually did not want to spend time with you, you may now find him gravitating toward you—which is to say that either way, a healthier balance will be achieved.

When he feels nourished by the marriage, there will be fewer complaints and less jealousy about your spending time with friends, taking a class, or whatever else your heart and soul need in order to replenish. He will be neither possessive nor reclusive when you are giving him what he really needs, which is to be cared for with abiding love and mercy. He will be more comfortable with or without you because he knows your love is steadfast and is therefore not dependent on your physical presence. In spending less time trying to control or worry about the nature of your relationship, you will have the time and temperament to take better care of your own needs, which is all-important.

If you allow extended time for just hanging out together with no agenda, your relationship will broaden and deepen. Through the generosity of your time, being fully present and listening, you may get to know the parts of him you have not observed before; he will be less guarded now that your critical self has all but disappeared. As you begin see him, you will begin to be seen.

You can start sharing your interests instead of keeping them all to yourself. Your activities may have been mostly foreign to him, and therefore seemingly not of interest, but as you reveal yourself through your stories, new ground for sharing will emerge. Because your marriage has become a stronger container of trust and love, you will each feel safer to reveal a bit more about what matters to you, knowing you will have a more appreciative and knowledgeable audience.

As your relationship issues ease up, you may notice a more subtle world. Now and then you may feel as if you are surrounded by a cloud of expansive softness—expansiveness because you are embracing all possibilities, and softness because your rough edges have worn down. You have dropped your sword and your shield and therefore do not invite attack. You have nothing to protect. You do not take yourself so seriously, but you have taken God's work very seriously. You have been merciful and kind *when it did not come easily.* You have let God's plans unfold. You have allowed yourself to be imperfect. You are free. You are happy and at peace. You are in love with all of creation. You are joyous and grateful knowing you can make a small contribution to goodness in the world and the world will smile back.

You are making a consistent, sincere effort to be loving, and God is grateful. You now realize that you are never alone, that God is ever present and is your Trusted Friend. You also trust that your husband is there for you in ways you never dreamed possible and will continue to be there for you for all time. Now you are ready and open to receive the love you so deserve.

Remember, you are *garments for one another.* Cloak him in the raiment of honor and dignity and he will do the same for you. Honor him, and he will begin to honor you.

A Prayer for You ...

*Dear Lord, the source of all compassion and
mercy, I cannot thank You enough for the
newfound love that is blossoming in my heart
and in my marriage. Thank you for your
patience with me and forgive me for the times
I did not see Your wisdom and goodness in
bringing to me the blessings of this marriage.
Thank you for the flow of your ever-present
forgiveness, guidance, and love even when
I turn away. Help me continue to open my
heart to allow Your loving-kindness to flow
freely through me.*

*I am forever needy of the beauty and
majesty of Your presence.*

Amen

11

Love, Mercy, and Forgiveness

L ove and forgiveness are inseparable. Set your intention to nurture love, and forgiveness will come your way. Set your intention to forgive, and your heart will open to love.

Forgiving self and forgiving others go hand and hand, for how can you extend to another what you yourself have not tasted? Allow yourself to feel the uninterrupted flow of mercy available to you and open your heart to let it in.*

We all ask for love and mercy and we aspire

---

*   Mercy, sometimes used interchangeably with forgiveness, is often described as forgiveness and compassion.

to give the same to others. We would like to be kinder, more appreciative, more forgiving in any situation. It is no easy task to walk in the world with grace, purity, love, and mercy, but we do so—some of the time.

That we have free choice is the kicker. We have the capacity to sink to the lowest of the low or rise above the angelic, even within a single day. This book has been about making choices that will optimize love and peace in your relationships—with God, others, and self. Almost certainly, you will have disappointments, setbacks that may seem all the more painful because of the efforts you have made and the heights you have reached. These will pass, leaving drops of wisdom in their wake. Learning to love is a lifelong journey—expect successes, wrong turns, and places of rest. Embrace it all and keep returning to the unlimited well of God's mercy and forgiveness.

Our spiritual walking is seldom in a straight line. Our lives are more like a never-ending series of ascending and descending arcs, like a roller coaster ride but one that can take us ever higher. We ascend, and our understanding of ourselves and our proximity to God increase. Then we descend, by choice or circumstance. We shed what no longer serves us, "untying the knots of our mind" so we can ascend again to fill our cups anew, with the greater understanding and competence we need to continue on our spiritual journey. Each cycle draws us ever closer to the peace, love, mercy, and holiness we are seeking.

> *Do not despair of the Mercy of Allah: verily He forgives all sins. Truly He is Oft-Forgiving, Most Merciful.*

> *Carry me on the swift noble mounts ... of Your deep love and Your tender mercy.... O Lord! Give us from Your presence, mercy and provide for us straightforwardness in our conduct.*

> *Surely goodness and mercy shall follow me all the days of my life.*

The Practice of Repentance

One of the most helpful tenets in all religions is some way to deal with regret and seek forgiveness. Otherwise our mistakes can pile up and veil us from the light of mercy.

Repentance (*tawbah*) is a mainstay of Sufism, a practice used at every step along the spiritual path. Although it is usually recited in Arabic, in English it would be the repeated chanting of *O Lord, please forgive me.*

Although the process of repentance comes from within, it is inspired by God sending mercy to us first. We usually aren't aware of receiving that mercy, except as it inspires in us a feeling of remorse. *Tawbah* is the state of regretting something we have done, or even something someone else has done if it has caused us to lose our connection to God. Yes, we even practice *tawbah* when someone else has hurt us, because we turned away from God in our judgement of their behavior.

Tawbah may also be invoked for its cleansing quality, with no specific transgression in mind, only the desire to come closer to God. Qualities for forgiveness may be chanted for states of confusion, indecision, doubt—anything that breaks our connection with God. In the process of *tawbah*, we return our negative thoughts and actions back to God, experience our deep regret, and vow to do better next time.

The first *tawbah*, it was said, was practiced by the angels for questioning God's wisdom in creating humans. "Will you place upon the earth one who will corrupt it … while it is we who hymn Your praise and sanctify You?" the angels said. "Truly I know what you know not," God replied, and then the angels repented for the first and last time.

> *Do not let your mistakes keep you from your Beloved but again and again wash in the water of forgiveness…. Through the gate of the mistake My beloveds come to reach Me. First I put them in the fire of the mistake,*

then this fire brings them to the deeper fire of My love. But learn and repent. Consume the essence of the mistake, so that once having done this and deeply understood, you cannot return to make that mistake again. Offer the essence of the mistake to Me in the fire of your love for Me, and My love for you, and do not take it back again.

God in His mercy sometimes hides from us mistakes we have made when the knowledge of our faults would be too much for us to bear at that time and therefore would be a hindrance, not a help, in our spiritual walking. *Tawbah*, which includes praying for forgiveness and/or chanting the qualities of forgiveness, is recommended as a daily practice, even when we are not certain what has come between us and God. Repentance is not a belittling of our self but rather an acknowledgement that there is no end to our desire to manifest our best self. We will always miss the mark. It is a relief to bare our fallibility before the One, acknowledging our neediness and feeling our gratitude for the opportunity to restore our connection, which *tawbah* provides. No matter how far we travel on our spiritual journey, repentance (*tawbah*) is with us always, for what may not seem to be in error now may well be noticeable when we have walked further on our spiritual path.

It deserves repeating that repentance comes

because God has *already* sent mercy and forgiveness. This mercy stirs our heart and causes us to feel regret, which opens us to receive the mercy being sent. So *tawbah* comes from God to us, not the other way around. The God-sent mercy sparks our regret, and we complete the circle with our apology, a returning, and a pledge to not repeat.

Just as God does for us, God covers up the mistakes of others when they are not yet ready to see them. When we see others doing what we think is wrong, we may judge them and want to point out to them the mistake they have made. However, knowing that God, out of His kindness and wisdom, has hidden from them the knowledge of their mistake, we can more easily allow that event to remain between them and God. In this case, as I mentioned in chapter 6, we can simply model correct behavior for the other and not shame them by pointing out their mistake.

The Divine Qualities of Mercy and Forgiveness

Remember, all the divine attributes are established inside each human, waiting to be awakened and perfected. Through reading these names, or even chanting them, you may begin to feel the resonance with that quality inside of you.

The ultimate quality of forgiveness, *Afuw,*

means complete forgiveness, such that "even the slightest traces of wounds and upsets vanish so that we do not retain any memory of them." This is the highest stage of divine forgiveness.

Another quality of forgiveness, mercy, and compassion is *Halim*, which is described as a

> *gentle, kind love that nurtures on the physical and emotional levels* ... Halim *brings a gentleness that soothes all anger, all impatience. Just like nature around us, it has an opening, pacifying magic that fills the heart with a peace and quiet that goes by the name of* Sakeena (Shekinah *in Hebrew), the peace that arises from being aware of God's presence* ...
>
> ... Halim *is as universal and all-embracing as the womb for the fetus.... Look at the earth. It carries everything—beauty and ugliness, heaviness and lightness, yet flowers and fragrances sprout from it. Such is the divine quality of* Halim.

Physicians of the Heart describes *Halim* in a reference to the patience required of the prophet Abraham regarding his father. It is said that he just sighed in response to his father's disagreement with his view of a singular God, even though it must have rocked him deeply.

A Practice: Sighing Through Discomfort

Sighing is a wonderful release for any uncomfortable emotion. Here is a short exercise for when our nerves get the best of us, or when we simply wish to feel more peaceful and more grounded: In rounds of three, take a long deep in-breath, followed by a slow and thorough exhalation and sounding of a-a-a-h-h. As we sigh, our whole body begins to relax, and we gently drop into deeper, quieter parts of our being.

> *Each sigh takes you into the deep abyss of your essence, to the dark and gentle place of your inner being. And there the Beloved is waiting. Back and forth you go between tenderness and fear. I am beyond my anger, I am beyond my hurt. I am beyond my pride; I am beyond my brokenness. I am waiting in the eternal peacefulness, and I know that in this infinite patience is the womb of creation. This is the feminine quality in the love of God.*

A Practice: Tasting a Quality

To taste a quality, to experience how the sound resonates with your heart, you can recite *"ya"* (meaning "Oh") and then the name. For example, *ya Halim, ya Halim, ya Halim, ya Halim*. Find a rhythm that pleases you, singing or simply saying the name. If you have a string of beads of any kind, use this to count a round of chanting. I recommend at least two hundred recitations, or fifteen minutes of reciting, with no other intention but to have a quiet awareness, remaining open to what may transpire.

12

Surrender

*And do not walk arrogantly upon
the earth. Surely you cannot tear the
earth apart, and you will never be
taller than the mountains.*

From your new place of being, you should not be surprised to find yourself feeling kinder and more grateful. Your experience of faith, love, and divine guidance is expanding, God willing.

Take time now to reflect on the changes in your marriage, however small. What ways of relating to your spouse do you hope to continue? Do you feel your efforts have been worth the trouble? Why or why not?

Did you stick with the plan for at least a month? If not, you might want to dedicate yourself to the suggestions given for a longer period. These are not short-term behaviors, but rather are designed to be lifelong patterns of relating: of giving unconditional love, consistently, as best you can.

A New Way of Being

Here is my hope for your experience. You have renewed your commitment to your marriage for the sake of God. You've learned new ways to be with your spouse, practiced them, and integrated them into your life. You more fully care for your spouse out of love, not fear, appearances, or duty begrudged. You have understood and applied some of the mystical teachings about men and women, about love, and about your divine self.

You have learned to recognize the pitfalls and see the warning signs of slipping back into your old ways. You have learned to care not only for your husband but for your relationship with God and the divine being that is your true essence.

You have begun to compost the field of your marriage with faith, kindness, humility, and love, and God is bestowing the sun of truth, the breeze of love, and the rain of mercy upon your precious heart.

Let this freedom that has come from surrendering your ego self in your marriage spread to all relationships. Make it a point to find someone you are in judgment of and determine to connect to them. Be caring and kind, accepting and interested, and be open for a transformation.

The Gifts of Humility

As was said by a true lover, "How many times has love broken the barriers of pride and the lover has ended without his pride; and the humility of the seeker of love is something of wonder."

Every challenge comes bearing a gift (Fa-ina mal usri usra).

One of the gifts among the challenges of marriage is the humility that comes from recognizing our complete powerlessness to create the outcomes we desire. Ironically, we will get what we need when we give up the reins of control and, in their stead, cultivate loving-kindness. From this place of deeper surrender, the understandings we so fervently seek may be delivered. Gnosis, our heart's longing, is an extraordinary gift from on High, coming in on the wings of Grace to those who draw closer.

*Live the richness and the kindness of your
true being: acquire knowledge, do good, be
kind to all living beings, and thus attain your
peace and your inner dignity.*

Our dignity does not come from demanding respect. Rather, it radiates from the essence of our being, thus inviting respect. It comes from the light we carry, a light whose origin is not our ego self. Dignity comes when we fully surrender all that we are to the One. It comes from the realization that without God we are nothing. In short, we become somebody when we realize we are nobody, when our *neediness* for God becomes so profound that we are brought to our knees. It is then that we are made noble by association. In humbling ourselves we find our dignity in God.

*It has been narrated that one of the Gnostics
said, I attempted to enter into the presence of
Allah from all of the doors of obedient acts,
but I would not come to a door without finding it overflowing and packed; so I could not
enter in. That was my state until I came to
the door of lowliness, humility, submission,
and indigence, and I found it to be the closest
and widest door to Him, with no crowding
and no obstacle; and no sooner had I placed
my foot in the threshold [than] did He Most*

High take me by the hand and enter me into
His presence.

We cannot make ourselves surrender our egos more fully, nor can we make ourselves more reverent. But we can ready the ground.

Bury your existence in the earth of obscurity,
For whatever sprouts forth,
Without having first been buried,
Flowers imperfectly.

Know your incapacity and powerlessness;
that He will give you of His power. So ask
to be taken by the hand and to be moved to
the presence of your Lord ... then your illu-
sions will be destroyed in the true under-
standing and your ignorance will become
true knowledge.

Let it be. Let it go. You have no real control. Let go of who you think you are that you may discover who you truly are. Let go of your opinions of what your spouse should be doing, or being. Let others make mistakes. Let yourself make mistakes. You don't have to be in charge any longer. This is the real freedom.

The weight of arrogance is such
that no bird can fly
carrying it.

You have nothing to give to God, really; nothing belongs to you. Your essential nature was inblown by your Lord. Your very breath is but a gift from God. Everything you are is by grace. When you recognize this, you naturally bow with a sense of awe for the majesty and beauty of all of creation, including your deepest self. This surrender leads you to a place of reverence and incredible neediness. Into this crater of neediness will flow God's abundance for you. Let your Lord carry you.

Where the lowland is, that's where
the water goes.
—Rumi

My guide Sidi ended one of his most widely read books with this amazing statement:

Indeed, God greatly loves the righteous god-
fearing hidden ones, who are not searched for
nor missed when they are absent, nor are they
noticed or recognized when they are present.
These are the leaders of guidance and the
torches of knowledge.

And he cautioned us, as well:

Do not be careless with the grace of proxim-
ity. Be aware of the truth of the nearness of
the unseen, like one who sits and serves in the
court of a perfect king. In the presence of the
king, do not profess yourself to have knowl-
edge because this knowledge is ignorance, and
do not profess yourself to be humble because
this humility is arrogance and vanity. Be
silent and realize where you stand.

We All Seek Contentment

Know that no one reaches the reality of
al-rida (contentment)
Except through patience with trials,
Gratitude in times of ease,
Reliance upon the Lord of the heaven,
Making sweet the bitterness of the decree
And being under the authority of the love
In what is pleasing and in what is difficult.

Love what your Beloved sends you.

You have accepted this gift from God, this
gift of your spouse. Because you accepted it and
allowed God's will to prevail, not yours, it was
transmuted into gold. A miracle has occurred.

Everything you needed in a partner was already in front of you.

You may think these travels have been just about your relationship to your spouse, but in fact all along it's been about your relationship with God. The gold at the end of this rainbow is more than a happy marriage, or greater ease with relationships in general. It is about your connection to God, and your accepting and surrendering to God's will. *Not my will but Thy will be done.* The peace and the joy, the understanding and the moral compass that come your way as a result of your efforts are priceless. Not only has your earthly relationship with your spouse been transformed, but your soul and your spirit have been transformed as well. When we are in deep surrender, God really does bring miracles.

As you are humbled, people will gravitate toward you and want to be with you because they unknowingly want what you carry. From your place of certainty, your presence creates no disturbance in the field; you ask for nothing, want for nothing, and have no agenda. You carry an indwelling peace, the *sakeenah* (Arabic).

Let go of being somebody. No one will notice. You will see the world through new eyes. People will see or feel your light and want to be with you, not because you are somebody but because of the light of goodness you carry inside. You will find comfort in the truth that you are but a part of the fabric of creation. You are no longer imprisoned by having to keep up appearances. Your only goal is to be an emissary of caring and goodness—a knower of love—for a God who is all merciful. Even your mistakes are a part of His grace.

I wish you well on your journey. No relationship is perfect. With God's help, your marriage will continually evolve, yielding greater and greater contentment, trust, love, and peace. Your trials and challenges with your spouse are a vital part of your walking. They will motivate you to continue strengthening your capacity to love and be loved. You are discovering an intimacy that comes from respect and humility in the face of the One Who gave you the blessing of this marriage. God willing, your efforts have contributed not only to harmony in your relationships but harmony in your being and harmony with God. When we set our intention, God collaborates with us and makes easier our efforts.

. . .

I'll leave you with a flood of words that awakened me one morning before first light:

Only when you leave the control room,
content to drift on the ocean of infinite mercy,
moved by the winds of divinity, choosing
right action over need to please or fear of

*displeasing, will you fully grasp the incred-
ible truth that God has arranged for you to
live with an amazing stranger, a unique and
barely known being, within whom countless
mysteries await to be revealed.*

*Be patient. How can you think you know
your husband when you are still excavating
and understanding your own being? The
best part of the journey begins with your
complete acceptance of him in every moment,
understanding that God is communicating
with you through him. Then, to your amaze-
ment, each day some new aspect of him will
be revealed, and because of the delight he sees
in your eyes, a growing desire to please you
will awaken.*

*You may sheepishly wonder why you
spent so long trying to transform your
husband into the mate you want, when all
along he is the mate you need—a divine gift
guaranteed to awaken deeply wonderful and
challenging places in you both.*

*Divine knowledge is so vast, so incom-
prehensible as to astound and confuse our
hearts and spirits. Who knew? you ask
yourself. Who knew that all of this, and more,*

was inside us both? Who knew that joy and contentment, companionship and steadfast presence were here to be mined, through the delicate instruments of love and mercy?

May peace and blessings be upon you and your marriage, always, and may God keep you close.
—Salima Linda

Appendix A:
Names for the One

*What are all these different names for
the same church of love we kneel in
together?*
St. Teresa of Avila

My intent is not to make separation among us. This book is foremost about helping us all be more loving. Whatever your background, I hope you will find some gems of inspiration within.

Recognizing that there may be issues with some words, I will address them, below.

There are many names used for that ineffable, infinite, mysterious One. I use the word *God* in this book because it is the most commonly used word. My preference is the Arabic word for God, *Allah*, which you may be surprised to learn is the word for God you would hear in Christian churches in Arabic-speaking countries. However, the word

Allah has some triggers associated with it, so in this book I chose to use God to reach a wider audience.

Allah is part of my Sufi tradition—*The God, Al Llah*. I like the way it opens my heart, like a sigh. Allah has a double aaahh sound, the vowel associated with the heart chakra, with a breathy "h" at the end. All Aramaic languages vibrate in our body, sending waves into all our cells. It is said that the sound precedes the meaning, something you may notice as you speak the qualities and know their meanings (see Appendix C). Jesus spoke Aramaic, also a language of sound, using a similar word for God, *Elaha.* It is also a heart opener, but it is not a language I know.

As you read, feel free to substitute whatever word connects you to your Lord, the One.

With regard to "He," a word used as the pronoun for God: unfortunately, there is no inclusive pronoun. I used to substitute *She* for *He* when reading, and still do on occasion. Of course, you are free to do the same.

In
My soul
There is a temple, a shrine, a mosque,
a church
where I kneel …
Rabia

Appendix B:
Poems of Surrender
and Grace

Letting Go, Letting God
Tiffany Hasna Wood

She let go.
Without a thought or a word,
she let go. She let go of the fear.
She let go of the judgments. She
let go of the confluence of
opinions swarming around her
... head. She let go of the committee
of indecision within her. She let
go of all the "right" reasons.
Wholly and completely, without
hesitation or worry, she just let go.

She didn't ask anyone for advice.
She didn't read a book on how to
let go. She didn't search the

scriptures. She just let go. She let
go of all the memories that held
her back. She let go of all the
anxiety that kept her from moving
forward. She let go of the
planning and all of the
calculations about how to
do it just right.

She didn't promise to let go. She
didn't journal about it. She didn't
write the projected date in her
Day-Timer. She made no public
announcement and put no ad in
the paper. She didn't check the
weather report or read her daily
horoscope. She just let go.

She didn't analyze whether she
should let go. She didn't call her
friends to discuss the matter. She
didn't do a five-step Spiritual
Mind Treatment. She didn't call
the prayer line. She didn't utter
one word. She just let go.

No one was around when it
happened. There was no
applause or congratulations. No
one thanked her or praised her.

No one noticed a thing. Like a
leaf falling from a tree, she just
let go. There was no effort. There
was no struggle. It wasn't good
and it wasn't bad. It was what it
was, and it is just that.

In the space of letting go, she let
it all be. A small smile came over
her face. A light breeze blew
through her. And the sun and the
moon shone forevermore.

Sufi Junkie (excerpt)
Published in *Love Knows Your Name*
Lanita Rahma Woller

... I am desperate, Allah, needy, lost.
You are the Mercy within my desperation,
The Light within my lostness,
The Love within my need.

The Garden Du'a
Maryam Helen Eccher

Who are you?
I heard a loving voice in the silence tell me
A gardener I shall be.

Where are you going?
To the garden of faith and love
Where flowers are blooming in the hearts of all.
What grows faith grows the flowers
It is the Divine gift of Grace
That arrives in a flash of holy flame
The essence of sun and moonlight
Reflected awe and beauty
In dew and teardrops that wash heart and soul
Revealing ever deeper flames of Grace
Flash of an angel's wing
Bees in flight to the queen mother
Messengers of the mystic silence of love
Showing the way to the Garden.

Dressed in Wonder and faithfulness
Knee deep in dahlias and roses
Carrying a full basket of water
Stepping into the garden, tending to 99 flowers[*]
Fragrant treasures of faith and love
Forgetfulness washed away
Divine remembrance is the noble feast of faith.

[*]   A reference to the 99 qualities, or aspects, of God.

Appendix C:
Introduction to
the Divine Qualities

The Divine Qualities are aspects of God that all humans embody and that are our life's work to explore and perfect. As you read through these qualities, contemplate that each one carries a possibility for you to better know yourself and God. Through our spiritual walking, whatever form it takes, we are in a sense purifying each inner quality so our understanding and manifestation of it become deeper and truer, acknowledging that the full and true template belongs to God alone.

God wanted to see Himself reflected in all of creation, and so He made that possible through the gift of the qualities. You will recognize these qualities as attributes that you and all of humanity are familiar with and capable of embodying to some degree, depending on whether the particular quality has been allowed to shine forth or has become twisted due to life events. In either case, your yearning to carry these divine qualities is always there. You may also recognize some, though not all, of these qualities in the rest of creation. You may observe that the plants, animals, and even rocks and other inanimate substances display their qualities in a purer fashion (for example, the steadfastness of rocks), which is both their attraction and their teaching for us.

If, wanting to know more, you were to search the Internet for the "ninety-nine names of God," you would notice that the various lists of qualities differ slightly from one another. Though more than ninety-nine names have been identified, each list contains only ninety-nine, the hundredth name being reserved for God. Following are some of the more familiar qualities.

Rahim: The Most Merciful
Rahman: The Most Compassionate
Quddus: The Most Holy
Salaam: The Source of Peace, Safety,
    and Wholeness
Jabbar: The Irresistible, the One
    Who Unites
Razzaq: The Provider
Alim: The All Knowing
Latif: The Subtle Tender One
Halim: The Clement
Ghafur: The All Forgiving

Hafiz: The One Who Preserves,
    Safeguards
Karim: The Generous
Hakim: The All Wise
Wadude: The Loving
Haqq: The Truth
Wakil: The Trustee
Matin: The Firm, the Unshakeable
Ghafur: The All-Forgiving
Waliyy: The Protective Friend
Hayy: The Living, the One
    Who Always Exists
Ahad: The One
Qadir: The Able
Barr: The Source of all Goodness
Tawwab: The Accepter of Forgiveness
Afuw: The Pardoner
Rauf: The Compassionate
Nur: The Divine Light
Hadi: The Guide
Sabur: The Patient

Clearly, these are attributes of *God*. We ourselves will never be the "the most compassionate,"
for example, but through our connection to and
reliance on God, we can develop this inner quality
more purely. Because some of our divine qualities
may have "rusted over," we say that recitation
polishes these qualities within us, enabling us to

mirror some of the qualities for others, to God's pleasure.

Reading about a quality is one way to discover its nuances and applicability. Recitation of a quality is another way to become familiar with a godly aspect in ourselves, in a way that our bodies can feel, retain, and return to. To recite one or more divine names repeatedly, silently or aloud, is to let our being be washed with that divine attribute, and so to experience that aspect of our true essence. Find a rhythm and volume that works for you, e.g., ya (Oh) Rahman ya Rahim, ya Rahman ya Rahim, ya Rahman ya Rahim, and be open to the experience without expectations. You may not feel the effects of your recitation right away, but over time results will come. Follow your inner guidance, and let your visits with these qualities move you closer to the truth you already know, to your home, your inner divine nature.

Notes

Introduction

Page

ix.   Respect other people's way … Rosina-Fawzia Al-Rawi, *Divine Names: The 99 Healing Names of the One Love* (Northampton, MA: Olive Branch Press, 2015), 301.

x.   Love is something … Malvina Reynolds, "Magic Penny."

xii.   Dear Lord, You are the Pen … Sidi Shaykh Muhammad Sa'id al-Jamal ar-Rifa'i ash-Shadhuli, *A Righteous Word Is Like a Righteous Tree* (Pope Valley, CA: Shadhiliyya Sufi Center, 2009), 281.

Chapter 1

3.   And join me to You … Sidi Shaykh Muhammad Sa'id al-Jamal ar-Rifa'i ash-Shadhuli, *Music of the Soul: Sufi Teachings* (Petaluma, CA: Sidi Muhammad Press, 1994), 262–63.

5.   Become kinder with every hour … Al-Rawi, *Divine Names*, 135.

5.   Know, my beloved … Muhammad al-Jamal ar-Rifa'i, *Music of the Soul*, 173.

Chapter 2

9.   That part of your life ... Victor Danner, *The Book of Wisdom* (New York: Paulist Press, 1978), 100.

11. When love beckons to you ... Kahlil Gibran, *The Prophet* (New York: Knopf, 1923), 11.

15. Truly I tell you ... Matthew 25:40.

17. You cannot separate ... Gibran, *The Prophet*, 41.

17. Things that happen to us ... Al-Rawi, *Divine Names*, 117.

18. When irritation comes ... See Salima Sanford, *Healing Your Marriage by Healing Yourself* (Mistletoe Press, 2022), chapter 3, for more.

19. Love is too powerful ... Sidi Shaykh Muhammad Sa'id al-Jamal ar-Rifa'i ash-Shadhuli, *The Path to Allah Most High* (Sidi Muhammad Press, 2007), 93.

Chapter 3

21. And ever has it been ... Gibran, *The Prophet*, 7.

22. O children of Adam ... Ibn Al-'Arabi, *101 Diamonds: From the Oral Tradition of the Glorious Messenger Muhammad*, Lex Hixon and Fariha al-Jerrahi, tr. (New York: Pir Press, 2002), 101.

28. You are the question ... Muhammad al-Jamal ar-Rifa'i, *Music of the Soul*, 19.

Chapter 4

35. The light on your face ... Sheikh Abu-Saeed Abil-Kheir, *Nobody, Son of Nobody: Renditions of Poems*, Vraje Abramian, tr. (Prescott, AZ: Hohm Press, 2001), 15.

35. The light that dispels ... Sidi Shaykh Muhammad Sa'id al-Jamal ar-Rifa'i, *The Meadow of Poetic Truths* (Sidi Muhammad Press, 2001), 114.

36. I was a Hidden Treasure ... An often quoted Sufi hadith.

37. The spirit of man ... Ibn Al-'Arabi, *The Ringstones of Wisdom*, Caner K. Dagli, tr. (Chicago: Kazi Publications, 2004), xxx.

37. It is the presences of the Names ... Al-'Arabi, *The Ringstones of Wisdom*, xxvi.

37. Love exists as a fundamental ... Sidi Shaykh Muhammad Sa'id al-Jamal ar-Rifa'i, *The Path of Yearning to Taste the Love* (Sidi Muhammad Press, 2021), 40.

38. You are the treasure ... Muhammad al-Jamal ar-Rifa'i, *Music of the Soul*, 71.

42. Like the ocean ... Gibran, *The Prophet*, 39.

44. Your task is not ... Jelalludin Rumi, Goodreads.

47. Yet God does not burden ... Qur'an 2:286.

48. I can raise my head ... Al-Rawi, *Divine Names*, 137–38.

48. So learn to forgive ... Al-Rawi, *Divine Names*, 75.

48. Be kind to those ... Al-Rawi, *Divine Names*, 78.

Chapter 5

49. Among the signs ... Danner, *The Book of Wisdom*, 42.

51. Respect other people's ways ... Al-Rawi, *Divine Names*, 301.

52. The soil of our mind ... Thich Nhat Hanh, Goodreads.

55. So love and keep loving ... Al-Rawi, *Divine Names*, 117.

59. Sometimes your joy ... Thich Nhat Hanh, Goodreads.

60. Hold fast unto the bond ... Qur'an 3:103.

61. The sun never says ... Hafiz, "The Sun Never Says" in *The Gift* (New York: Penguin, 1999), 34.

62. Being grateful brings ... Al-Rawi, *Divine Names*, 139.

63. Soft words soften hearts ... Islam Explorer website.

63. They Can Be Like the Sun ... "They Can Be Like the Sun," from Daniel Ladinsky, *Love Poems from God* (New York: Penguin, 2002), 324.

64. O God, I take refuge ... Ibn Al-'Arabi, *The Seven Days of the Heart: Prayers for the Nights and Days of the Week*, Pablo Beneito and Stephen Hirtenstein, tr. (Oxford, UK: Anqa Publishing, 2000), 66.

64. Every utterance ... Danner, *The Book of Wisdom*, 93.

66. Ra'uf awakens ... Al-Rawi, *Divine Names*, 300.

Chapter 6

71. You are the way ... Gibran, *The Prophet*, 40.

72. When you are angry ... See Sanford, *Healing Your Marriage by Healing Yourself*, 21–28.

73. When another person ... Thich Nhat Hanh, Goodreads.

75. The gratefulness of the earth ... Al-Rawi, *Divine Names*, 141.

77. Her emotions related ... Qur'an 94:5–6.

79. To get what you love ... Imam Al-Ghazali, azquotes.com.

79. If you see a person ... Paraphrased and directly quoted from Muhammad al-Jamal ar-Rifa'i, *Music of the Soul*, 220.

81. Be gentle and loving ... See Sanford, *Healing Your Marriage by Healing Yourself*, 85–87.

82. These unresolved issues ... See Robert Ibrahim Jaffe, *God's Way: Discover the Inner Meaning of Illness and the True Source of Healing* (Pasadena, CA: Best Seller Publishing, 2021).

85. There is nothing wrong ... Al-Rawi, *Divine Names*, 263–64.

Chapter 7

89. Do not lose hope ... Danner, *The Book of Wisdom*, 102.

91. Or, if it is a behavior ... See Sanford, *Healing Your Marriage by Healing Yourself*, 65–71, for more.

94. Let it be ... See Appendix B for the related poem by Tiffany Hasna Wood, "Letting God, Letting God."

96. Tenderly I now touch ... Ladinsky, *Love Poems from God*, 325.

102. Latif refines the veils ... Al-Rawi, *Divine Names*, 125, 126.

103. We beseech Your tender mercy ... *Hizbu-l-Lutf: Orison of Tender Mercy* (Green Mountain Branch, VA: Shadhdhuli School, 2000), 42.

Chapter 8

107. He knew you would not ... Danner, *The Book of Wisdom*, 104.

109. The path is love ... Al-Rawi, *Divine Names*, 13.

109. For everything there is a polish ... Charles Le Gai
     Eaton, *The Book of Hadith: Sayings of the Prophet
     Muhammad from the Mishkat al Masabih* (Watson-
     ville, CA, and Bristol, UK: The Book Foundation,
     2008), 67.

109. God is closer ... Qur'an 50:16.

110. Sometimes lights come upon you ... Danner, *The
     Book of Wisdom*, 99.

111. Actions are lifeless forms ... Danner, *The Book of
     Wisdom*, 48.

112. When he loosens ... Danner, *The Book of Wisdom*,
     72.

114. To know that the answer ... Al-Rawi, *Divine Names*,
     169.

Chapter 9

115. Because the essences ... Muhammad al-Jamal ar-
     Rifa'i, *The Path to Allah Most High*, 75.

116. Through love, we dissolve ... Al-Rawi, *Divine
     Names*, 66.

117. Therefore, Adam bends ... Muhammad al-Jamal
     Rifa'i, *The Path to Allah Most High*, 75.

118. Hence for man ... Paraphrase from Ibn Al-'Arabi,
     The Bezels of Wisdom, R. W. J. Austin, tr. (New York:
     Paulist Press, 1980), 270.

122. Listen to what is said ... Qur'an 39:18.

126. They can be like a sun ... Ladinsky, *Love Poems
     from God*, 324.

126. In the Old Testament ... Genesis 1:3.

126. He but says unto a thing ... Qur'an 2:82.

127. Those who forgive others ... Al-Rawi, *Divine Names*, 75.

129. The level of mercy ... See end of Part I, divine quality, page 66.

131. When love's voice beckons to you ... Gibran, *The Prophet*, 11.

Chapter 10

135. They [your wives] ... Qur'an 2:187.

140. Remember, you are garments ... Qur'an 2:187.

Chapter 11

144. Untying the knots of our mind ... Al-Rawi, *Divine Names*, 55.

145. Do not despair ... Qur'an 39:53.

145. Carry me on the swift ... Muhammad al-Jamal ar-Rifa'i, *Music of the Soul*, 258 and 264.

145. Surely goodness and mercy ... Psalm 23:6.

146. Will you place upon the earth ... Qur'an 2:30.

146. Truly I know ... Qur'an 2:30.

146. Do not let your mistakes ... Muhammad al-Jamal ar-Rifa'i, *Music of the Soul*, 133–34.

148. The God-sent mercy ... Sidi Shaykh Muhammad Sa'id al-Jamal ar-Rifa'i, *How the Arrival Is Realized: O People of Hearts and Souls and Intellects* (Sidi Muhammad Press, 2004), 129–37. This concept of *Tawbah* being *from* God is the chapter on Repentence.

149. The ultimate quality ... Al-Rawi, *Divine Names*, 295.

149. gentle, kind love ... Al-Rawi, *Divine Names*, 131–32.

149. *Physicians of the Heart* ... Wali Ali Meyer, Bilal Hyde, Faisal Muqaddam, Shabda Kahn, *Physicians of the Heart: A Sufi View of the 99 Names of Allah* (Sufi Ruhaniat International, 2011), 88–89.

150. Each sigh takes you ... *Physicians of the Heart*, 89.

Chapter 12

153. And do not walk arrogantly ... Qur'an 17:37.

155. As was said ... Sidi Shaykh Muhammad Sa'id al-Jamal ar-Rifa'i ash-Shadhuli, *The Taste of the Love* (Sidi Muhammad Press, 1998), 15.

155. Every challenge comes ... Qur'an 94:5.

156. Live the richness ... Al-Rawi, *Divine Names*, 248.

156. It hs been narrated ... Muhammad al-Jamal ar-Rifa'i, *How the Arrival Is Realized*, 170–71.

157. Bury your existence ... Danner, *The Book of Wisdom*, 49.

157. Know your incapacity ... Muhammad al-Jamal ar-Rifa'i, *Music of the Soul*, 362–63.

158. The weight of arrogance ... St. John of the Cross in Ladinsky, *Love Poems from God*, 320.

158. Where the lowland is ... Rumi, Goodreads.

158. Indeed, God greatly loves... Muhammad al-Jamal ar-Rifa'i, *How the Arrival Is Realized*, 186.

159. Do not be careless ... Muhammad al-Jamal ar-Rifa'i, *Music of the Soul*, 157.

159. Know that no one ... Muhammad al-Jamal ar-Rifa'i, *The Path to Allah Most High*, 227.

Appendix A

165. What are all these different names ... Excerpt from "Where the Holy Thaws" in Ladinsky, *Love Poems from God*, 290.

166. In my soul ... Excerpt from "In My Soul" in Ladinsky, *Love Poems from God*, 11.

Bibliography

Abil-Kheir, Sheikh Abu-Saeed. *Nobody, Son of Nobody: Renditions of Poems.* Tr. Vraje Abramian. Prescott, AZ: Hohm Press, 2001.

Al-'Arabi, Ibn. *The Bezels of Wisdom.* Tr. R. W. J. Austin. New York: Paulist Press, 1980.

———. *101 Diamonds: From the Oral Tradition of the Glorious Messenger Muhammad.* Tr. Lex Hixon and Fariha al-Jerrahi. New York: Pir Press, 2002.

———. *The Ringstones of Wisdom.* Tr. Caner K. Dagli. Chicago: Kazi Publications, 2004.

———. *The Seven Days of the Heart: Prayers for the Nights and Days of the Week.* Tr. Pablo Beneito and Stephen Hirtenstein. Oxford, UK: Anqa Publishing, 2000.

Al-Rawi, Rosina-Fawzia. *Divine Names: The 99 Healing Names of the One Love.* Northampton, MA: Olive Branch Press, 2015.

Ar-Rifa'i, Sidi Shaykh Muhammad Sa'id al-Jamal. *How the Arrival Is Realized: O People of Hearts and Souls and Intellects.* Sidi Muhammad Press, 2004.

———. *The Meadow of Poetic Truths.* Sidi Muhammad Press, 2001.

———. *The Migration of the Truthful Traveler.* Sidi Muhammad Prress, 2010.

————. *Music of the Soul: Sufi Teachings*. Petaluma, CA: Sidi Muhammad Press, 1994.

————. *The Path of Yearning to Taste the Love*. Sidi Muhammad Press, 2021.

————. *The Path to Allah Most High*. Sidi Muhammad Press, 2007.

————. *A Righteous Word Is Like a Righteous Tree*. Pope Valley, CA: Shadhiliyya Sufi Center, 2009.

————. *The Taste of the Love*. Sidi Muhammad Press, 1998.

Danner, Victor. *The Book of Wisdom*. New York: Paulist Press, 1978.

Eaton, Charles Le Gai. *The Book of Hadith: Sayings of the Prophet Muhammad from the Mishkat al Masabih*. Watsonville, CA, and Bristol, UK: The Book Foundation, 2008.

Gibran, Kahlil. *The Prophet*. New York: Knopf, 1923.

Hafiz. *The Gift*. Renderings by Daniel Ladinsky. New York: Penguin, 1999.

Hizbu-l-Lutf : Orison of Tender Mercy. Green Mountain Branch, VA: Shadhdhuli School, 2000.

Jaffe, Robert Ibrahim. *God's Way: Discover the Inner Meaning of Illness and the True Source of Healing*. Pasadena, CA: Best Seller Publishing, 2021.

Ladinsky, Daniel. *Love Poems from God*. New York: Penguin, 2002.

Meyer, Wali Ali, Bilal Hyde, Faisal Muqaddam, Shabda Kahn. *Physicians of the Heart: A Sufi View of the 99 Names of Allah*. Sufi Ruhaniat International, 2011.

Reynolds, Malvina. "Magic Penny." Copyright 1955 and 1958 Northern Music Corporation, renewed 1986.

Sanford, Salima. *Healing Your Marriage by Healing Yourself*. Mistletoe Press, 2022.

Gratitude

I am in deep gratitude to my editors, Sheridan McCarthy and Stanton Nelson of Meadowlark Publishing Services, who midwifed this book and have been a complete joy to work with. They speak the truth when they say that a really good collaboration is fueled by love, love among the collaborators and love of the work they're creating. I am thankful to Rosina-Fawzia al-Rawi for giving me permission to quote extensively from her exquisite book *Divine Names: The 99 Healing Names of the One Love.* I greatly appreciate Amina al-Jamal for allowing me to share quotes from the numerous books by our shaykh Sidi that she has published through Sidi Muhammad Press. I have been blessed with the support of my fellow teachers and classmates, but there are two whose help really stands out: Yasmine Rahmana Cindy Libman, who has given me encouragement and spiritual support every step of the way, as well as weighing in on the artwork for the book, and Judith Sharifa Keith, who has been there for me at every critical junction in my spiritual walking, always challenging me to go deeper. I am grateful to my two incredible teachers, Murshids in our Sufi community, Dr. Robert Jaffe and Salima Adelstein, whose wisdom and care have contributed enormously to my self-understanding and deeper connection with God. And finally, I am ever grateful to my husband, Graham, whose steadfastness and uprightness are a constant in my life. I am in daily gratitude to God in His wisdom for bringing us together. Were it not for the discord and diversity in our marriage, we might never have found the patience, gratitude, forgiveness, and love we now so enjoy.

About the Author

Salima Linda holds a Masters of Divinity degree from the University of Spiritual Healing and Sufism (2009). She is a respected Muqqadim Murabbi in her Shadhdhuliyyah Sufi community, and through her teachings and healings, is connected to people of faith in many parts of the world.

Currently a core teacher at the Institute of Spiritual Healing, she is also a certified Master Healer, a graduate of Dr. Ibrahim Jaffe's training. Utilizing the experience gained in her decade of practice she is able to help others move through the doorway of each challenge into greater peace, love, understanding, and connection to God.

Salima is also the author of *Healing Your Marriage by Healing Yourself* and is devoted to the topic of peace in marriage. Her Sufi name is derived from the quality Salaam, meaning peace, safety, and wholeness. Salim is often translated as "river of peace," a quality she naturally carries.

Mother and Sons

Poems and Essays

Laura Ibanez
Victor Ronald Ibanez
Carlos Rodrigo Maglalang

ARPress
ILLUMINATING IDEAS.
EMPOWERING VOICES

ARPress
45 Dan Road Suite 5
Canton MA 02021

Hotline: 1(888) 821-0229
Fax: 1(508) 545-7580

Ordering Information:
Quantity sales. Special discounts are available on quantity purchases by corporations, associations, and others. For details, contact the publisher at the address above.

Printed in the United States of America.

ISBN-13:   Softcover   979-8-89356-265-1
              eBook   979-8-89356-264-4

Library of Congress Control Number: 2024903358